FASHION 101

First published in 2008 by
Zest Books, an imprint of Orange Avenue Publishing
35 Stillman Street, Suite 121, San Francisco, CA 94107
www.zestbooks.net

Created and produced by Zest Books, San Francisco, CA
© 2008 by Orange Avenue Publishing LLC
Illustrations © 2008 by Ariel Krietzman

Text set in MrsEaves and Rotis Sans Serif; title text set in EquipoizeSans

Fashion

Library of Congress Control Number: 2007939159
ISBN-13: 978-0-9790173-4-6
ISBN-10: 0-9790173-4-3

CREDITS
EDITORIAL DIRECTOR: Karen Macklin
CREATIVE DIRECTOR: Hallie Warshaw
WRITER: Erika Stalder
EDITOR: Karen Macklin
ILLUSTRATOR: Ariel Krietzman
COVER DESIGN: Tanya Napier
PRODUCTION ARTIST: Cari McLaughlin
TEEN ADVISORY BOARD: Carolyn Hou, Maxfield J. Peterson, Joe Pinsker, Hannah Shr

Printed in China.
First printing, 2008
10 9 8 7 6 5 4 3 2 1

Every effort has been made to ensure that the information presented is accurate. Readers are strongly advised to read product labels, follow manufacturers' instructions, and heed warnings. The publisher disclaims any liability for injuries, losses, untoward results, or any other damages that may result from the use of the information in this book.

FASHION 101

A CRASH COURSE IN CLOTHING

ERIKA STALDER

ILLUSTRATIONS BY ARIEL KRIETZMAN

 ZEST BOOKS

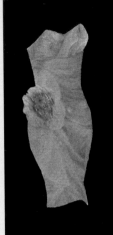

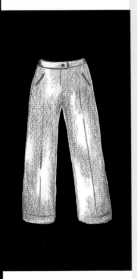

Clothes are such an integral part of our lives. Each year, we spend hours upon hours shopping and getting dressed, but do we ever actually think about what we're wearing? For example, what's the name of the style of your shirt? Who invented your favorite type of pants? Or who made your baby-doll nightie famous?

Typically, people look at what's hanging in their closet and see just clothes. Little do they know, there is a story behind every style. This book will reveal those stories. In *Fashion 101*, you'll learn where the miniskirt came from, why military outfitters and wartime restrictions have had a stronger influence on fashion than either Audrey Hepburn or Gwen Stefani, and how denim makers work those perfect "whiskers" into your "worn-out" jeans.

Are you a daring fashionista with a penchant for racy *hot pants*? Find out who was crazy enough to invent them and which working women were required to wear them as uniforms (no, not exotic dancers). Maybe you're just getting into this fashion thing. You'll pick up style tips that can help you avoid rookie moves like flashing VPL (short for visible panty lines).

Offering the total scoop on *underwear*, *outerwear*, and dozens of *accessories*, *Fashion 101* is a crash course in fashion that will guide you in how to put together smarter looks and become a fashion expert in the process.

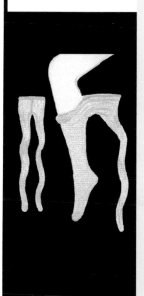

DRESSES AND SKIRTS
From Frocks and Smocks to Full Regalia

As recent as 80 years ago, women wore a dress or skirt every day. Can you imagine? Of course, our foremothers didn't have much choice: At that point, a woman's right to vote in the United States had not yet been recognized, much less the kind of gender-bending chic modeled by silver screen icon Marlene Dietrich. But with more freedom and physical activity came other types of garments, and the onetime bound-by-corset uniform is now a feminine power tool, worn when a girl wants to show off her silhouette and ladylike ways.

Consider the shifts Jackie Kennedy wore on the campaign trail; the backless, second-skin gown Marilyn Monroe slinked in while scandalously singing to JFK; or the shocking Versace bondage dress that Liz Hurley flaunted at the premiere of *Four Weddings and a Funeral*.

Even the most basic dress and skirt styles continue to prove timeless. Just check out the vintage gowns that A-list stars wear to big events—like the black-and-white Valentino Julia Roberts wore when she won her Academy Award. And since its introduction, the flirty miniskirt is yet to waver in popularity. Even the ball gown, which might seem dated at first glance (when was the last time you donned a crinoline under a floor-length gown?), has its very relevant and modern incarnation: the prom dress.

Many of life's milestones—quinceañeras, sweet sixteens, confirmations, Bar and Bat Mitvahs, weddings, and even graduations—are marked by the ritualistic wearing of a special gown. Gliding across the room in that perfect dress or skirt can make us feel like the star of the party—which is, after all, the point.

CHAPTER GLOSSARY

bias cut ❷ fabrics cut on the bias are cut diagonally across the grain of the fabric. **Slip dresses** are often cut on the bias. This cut is particularly flattering because it allows the fabric to hang smoothly rather than bunch or ride up on the body.

bodice ❷ section of a dress between the shoulders and the waistline.

cinch waist ❷ a waistline that is pulled in, generally with a belt.

dart ❷ a V-shaped taper sewn in a garment to make it fit closer to the body; in dresses, darts are often sewn into the bodice near the armpit.

décolleté ❷ a low-cut neckline.

dropped waist ❷ a waistline that falls below the natural waist.

empire waist ❷ a raised waistline that starts under the bust.

smocking ❷ a line of closely pinched fabric.

tapered ❷ becomes narrower at one end.

DRESS FABRICS GLOSSARY

brocade ❷ heavy silk fabric with patterns woven in silver- or gold-colored thread.

chiffon ❷ sheer, light fabric that's woven from silk, rayon, or wool.

cotton ❷ fabric woven from the natural fibers of the cotton plant.

duchesse satin ❷ unlike the slippery satin used in bed sheets and formal gowns, this satin is firm and holds a shape. Like taffeta, it's made from silk.

georgette ❷ sheer polyester and silk blend fabric with a crepe (crinkled) surface.

jersey ❷ knit fabric with elastic properties made from wool, silk, cotton, or rayon. Originally made on the Isle of Jersey off the English coast, where it was used to make clothing for fishermen. This fabric is notorious for its wrinkle-resistant properties. It wears and travels well.

Lycra ❷ DuPont's trademarked name for its spandex fiber.

microfiber ❷ lightweight, silky fabric made from a superfine polyester filament yarn.

organza ❷ sheer, rib-free fabric made from silk, nylon, rayon, or polyester similar to chiffon, but heavier and crisp.

rayon ❷ soft artificial silk made from cellulose. Rayon was first used in "silk" stockings, which debuted in 1912.

silk ❷ soft fabric made from threads produced by insect larvae.

spandex ❷ lightweight, strong, elastic synthetic fiber made from polyurethane.

taffeta ❷ smooth, shiny fabric made from silk. Its color, texture, and shine are the same on both sides. It has a fine weave like that of chiffon but holds shape. Often used in **pouf dresses**.

DRESSES

A-LINE DRESS

A-Line Dress

WHAT IT LOOKS LIKE:
"A-line" simply refers to the triangular shape of this dress, which is usually made from one piece of cloth that flares out from just below the bust to the bottom hem. The A can begin just under the bust (an empire waist-line) or at the hips (a dropped waistline).

WHO MADE IT: Christian Dior first showed it to the public in his spring 1955 line.

WHO MADE IT HOT: Dancing go-go girls and mod squaders in swinging London made a short version of the A-line one of the most sought-after styles of the 1960s.

HOW TO ROCK IT: The A-line shape looks great on lots of body types and with lots of different shoe styles. Wear it with **slipper flats**, **strappy sandals**, or **platforms**, depending on the style and fabric of the dress.

The A-Z on the A-Line

A-line dresses reached their height of popularity in the 1960s, but Dior's dress-by-letters inspiration didn't stop there. He also created the H-line (a more boxy cut) and the Y-line (a more tapered cut), both of which resemble the shapes of those letters. The most extreme A-line dress? The **trapeze dress**. Introduced by Yves Saint Laurent (who was designing for Dior), it has enough yardage to smack a twirling girl in the face.

APRON DRESS

WHAT IT LOOKS LIKE: Most apron dresses feature a wrap style and thick straps, and some are even open in the back, like a kitchen apron.

WHO MADE IT: The apron dress can be traced back to ancient times, when Egyptian rulers wore jewel-encrusted aprons not for cooking or cleaning but as part of their elaborate everyday ensembles. One could tell the wearer's rank of power based on the shape and placement of the apron's sparkling embellishments. Thousands of years later, in the 1920s, one of the first modern-day apron dresses was made; it was a full apron that covered the whole body and hung loosely like a smock.

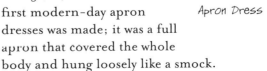
Apron Dress

WHO MADE IT HOT: Minnie Mouse, Julie Andrews in *The Sound of Music*, and the robo-hostesses from the 1975 and 2004 films *The Stepford Wives* all sported this whimsical take on homemaker fashion. The apron dress resurged in popularity with the new-school hippies of the '90s, who made a backless version out of patchwork corduroy and paired it with baggy jeans.

HOW TO ROCK IT: If you're daring, wear the backless version alone as a playful summer dress. If you don't want to show *that* much skin (or acquire funky tan lines), try layering it over a peasant skirt and cotton **camisole.**

BABY-DOLL DRESS

WHAT IT LOOKS LIKE: A nod to the nighties of the 1950s, the baby-doll dress is generally an empire-waisted frock with a low, scooped neckline, short sleeves, a loose fit, and a hemline that hits above the knee. Other variations include longer hemlines, dropped waists, long sleeves, and/or floppy collars. Because the full skirt allows the dress to move in a playful swing, soft and sheer fabrics like chiffon, rayon, and georgette are commonly used. Floral prints, stretch velvet, stretch lace, and sticky-sweet pastels are popular for this style, too.

WHO MADE IT: Mary Quant and other streetwear designers catering to the '60s teens of the youthquake (see right) brought baby dolls to the masses.

Baby-Doll Dress

WHO MADE IT HOT: Courtney Love and designers Anna Sui and Marc Jacobs helped make this style a wardrobe essential in the grunge-fueled 1990s. Their versions were often paired with rugged **combat boots**, like Doc Martens.

HOW TO ROCK IT: Toughen up the baby doll by wearing it with **leggings**, bodysuits, and combat boots. For a sweeter look, pair it with **ballerina flats** or **Mary Janes.**

The Shake of Youthquake

The 1960s were all about revolution—the birth of the women's liberation movement, the fight for civil rights, and the protests against the Vietnam War. It makes sense then that fashion also underwent a revolution during this time. Up until the '60s, girls pretty much wore whatever was handed down to them. But trends began moving the other way—bubbling up on the street and flowing into the French fashion houses. Gone were the refined hat-glove-dress ensembles and with them the stuffy authority of their makers. Instead, small-time, youth-run boutiques in London, and then in New York and San Francisco, served as launching pads for fresh, hip looks like **go-go boots**, loud prints, and, of course, the **miniskirt**. Even miniskirt maker Mary Quant knew there was a limit to what she could take credit for. "It wasn't me or Courrèges who invented the miniskirt," she said, "it was the girls in the street."

BALL GOWN

WHAT IT LOOKS LIKE: This long gown's signature attributes are a full skirt, a fitted bodice, and a low neckline. Layers of tulle are often built in under the skirt, and the hemline is usually floor-length to give the illusion that the woman is gliding or floating across the floor when she dances. This gown is always made of fabrics that hold shape, like taffeta and organza.

Ball Gown

WHO MADE IT: The ball gown dates back to the Middle Ages, when society's upper echelons attended formal dances. The 1850s saw a resurgence in this practice, which brought with it the resurgence of the gown. Today's equivalent, the prom or quinceañera dress, is most famously produced by Jessica McClintock.

WHO MADE IT HOT: The most famous ball gown of them all? Cinderella's of course.

HOW TO ROCK IT: Because most ball gowns have a low décolleté, upswept hair helps elongate and draw more attention to the neck.

BUBBLE DRESS

WHAT IT LOOKS LIKE: Any dress that features a tapered hemline can be considered a bubble. This technique causes a billowing, ballooning look instead of a hard edge.

WHO MADE IT: Pierre Cardin created the bubble dress and skirt in 1957. The style's lineage continued with Zandra Rhodes' elasticized bubble hemlines in the '70s and the ubiquitous **pouf dress** of the next decade. The more modern bubble dress provides similar volume, but is more low-key and takes up much less space.

WHO MADE IT HOT: The bubble look—in dress, skirt, and shirt form—has been seen in the past few years on nearly every Hollywood starlet, from Jessica Alba to Kate Beckinsale.

Bubble Dress

HOW TO ROCK IT: The bubble dress looks best when made from material that holds shape, like microfiber instead of limp cotton. Pair a bubble dress with a cashmere **cardigan** and flats for a modern-day princess effect that's more Lauren Conrad than Sleeping Beauty.

How the Belle of the Ball Kept It Clean

Ever wonder why traditional ball gowns have *so* much volume from the waist down? The original reason, established back in the mid-1800s, was to keep single guys at a respectable distance from sought-after ladies dancing at formal balls. It took more than a century for the mountains of layers to disappear from formal dress, and for attire more suitable for dirty dancing to surface.

CAFTAN

WHAT IT LOOKS LIKE:
Traditionally, this is an
ankle-length tunic gown
with wide sleeves and
an open neckline. Mod-
ern versions often have
higher hemlines, empire
waists, and/or narrower
sleeves. Caftans are usually
made of lightweight and
somewhat stiff fabrics like
muslin, cotton, or linen,
though sometimes they're
also cut from silk.

Caftan

WHO MADE IT: This roomy,
straight-cut garment is based
on the traditional garb of North African and
Eastern Mediterranean men. In the 1950s,
Christian Dior first sent caftans down the
runway. Halston and Yves Saint Laurent
followed a few years later.

WHO MADE IT HOT: This style was famously
worn by 1960s jet-setters like former *Vogue*
editor Diana Vreeland, socialite Babe Paley,
and heiress Barbara Hutton. Barbra Streisand
and Elizabeth Taylor also helped the caftan go
from traditional dress for men to chic clothing
for women.

HOW TO ROCK IT: If the caftan had an address,
it would be Leisureland USA; it's always been a
resort wear staple and favorite beach cover-up.
To get the look of relaxation, pair it with **flat-
soled sandals** or go totally barefoot.

CHEONGSAM
(AKA QUIPAOS)

WHAT IT LOOKS LIKE: A traditional Chinese
gown (pronounced "chong-som") made of
embroidered brocade fabric, the cheongsam has
a stand-up collar with a button closure on the
right side of the neck and a body-skimming fit
like the **sheath dress**.

WHO MADE IT: Chinese men first wore the
loose-fitting cheongsam about 500 years ago,
but the cheongsam look was eventually adopted
by Westerners who altered the style for women.
By the 1950s, the new, Western-influenced
cheongsam was more **shift**like, with a daring
slit up the side.

WHO MADE IT HOT: Calendar
girls of the 1930s first introduced the cheongsam to
the Western masses. This
dress took center stage in
the 1960 movie *The World of
Suzie Wong*.

HOW TO ROCK IT: The
cheongsam begs for up-
swept hair to show off the
dress's unique collar.

Cheongsam
(AKA Quipaos)

14

COATDRESS

Coatdress

WHAT IT LOOKS LIKE:
This dress is tailored a lot like an overcoat, with a collar, button-front closure, cuffs, and sometimes a sash at the waist. But it's more fitted to the body than a coat and is frequently made of heavy cotton with a hemline near the knees.

WHO MADE IT: The long coatdress was invented during WWI, but it wasn't until the '60s that it became a popular look for hipster women.

WHO MADE IT HOT: Though the Mary Poppins-type coatdress is possibly the most iconic, trench-style coatdresses have also been made popular by designers like Rachel Roy and Isaac Mizrahi. Princess Diana, a timeless style queen, is known to have been buried in a long, black Catherine Walker coatdress.

HOW TO ROCK IT: Wear an above-the-knee coatdress with superhigh heels and undo a couple of buttons at the top, like Cameron Diaz did at the 2007 *Vanity Fair* Oscar party.

COCKTAIL DRESS

WHAT IT LOOKS LIKE: Almost any simply styled formal dress can be dubbed a cocktail dress, but the typical cocktail is a short, often tight-fitting dress made of luxury fabrics like velvet, silk, satin, and silk jersey.

Cocktail Dress

WHO MADE IT: Cocktail culture emerged in the 1920s, when people began to host pre-dinner parties and needed something to wear to such events. As a result, designers created this streamlined yet saucy dress. Though he was not the first to create a cocktail dress, Christian Dior gave this easy and sophisticated frock its name.

WHO MADE IT HOT: Julia Roberts famously went searching for proper attire to wear on a night out in *Pretty Woman*. "I got a dress," she proudly told Richard Gere. "A cocktail one."

HOW TO ROCK IT: Though once worn with gloves and a hat, the modern-day cocktail dress works best with a nice pair of heels.

EMPIRE DRESS

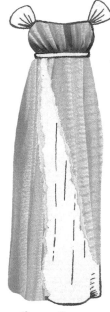

Empire Dress

WHAT IT LOOKS LIKE: The empire is a floor-length gown with a waistline just under the bust and a slim, column-style skirt that fits close to the body.

WHO MADE IT: This dress is named for the historical period in which it first became popular—the 1800s, during France's First Empire. The style has endured throughout the centuries, with popular revivals in the 1930s and '70s. Oftentimes the empire dress is adorned with Greek symbolism, like the classic Greek key pattern.

WHO MADE IT HOT: Rumor has it that Joséphine Bonaparte (who married Napoléon to become the first empress of the French) invented the style to disguise her pregnant belly. Whether or not that's true, she did become one of the style's first famed icons. Gwyneth Paltrow put a fresh face on the empire dress in her Oscar-winning role as Viola in 1998's *Shakespeare in Love*.

HOW TO ROCK IT: The straight columnar lines of this dress work best with simple shoes and accessories. To get the Spartan look of Queen Gorgo in *300*, pair it with dressy sandals, pulled-back hair, and dangling earrings.

JUMPER DRESS
(AKA PINAFORE)

WHAT IT LOOKS LIKE: The jumper is a sleeveless, loose-fitting dress worn over a boatneck long-sleeved shirt—like an old-school Brownie uniform.

WHO MADE IT: Its origins are hard to trace, but it appears that the jumper came onto the American radar through the works of early 20th-century designers like Coco Chanel and Paul Poiret, who made women's sportswear that consisted of two-piece outfits and closely resembled the modern-day jumper.

Jumper Dress (AKA Pinafore)

WHO MADE IT HOT: The traditional jumper brings to mind soccer moms and schoolmarms, but the fabulously flirty dresses that Twiggy wore—the A-line minidress, the **trapeze dress**, and the **smock dress**—all draw from the jumper's loose-fitting structure.

HOW TO ROCK IT: Since jumpers tend to have gaping armholes and a loose fit, they go best with some kind of shirt underneath. Whether you make it racy in lace or wholesome in cotton pique is up to you.

KIMONO

WHAT IT LOOKS LIKE: Like a **T-shirt**, a kimono is formed in a T shape. It's cut from a single piece of cloth and wraps across the body with a sash, like a robe. Its sleeves are long and ultrawide.

Kimono

WHO MADE IT: The kimono is a traditional style of Japanese dress; fine tailors dating back to the eighth century have been making kimonos.

WHO MADE IT HOT: Fashion designers streamlined the shape of the kimono by minimizing its sleeve openings and losing the wrap style and sash tie. More recently, Madonna's first fashion line, M by Madonna for H&M, featured a fast-selling kimono dress.

HOW TO ROCK IT: When wearing a kimono, resist going overboard with Asian-inspired accessories, like teahouse slippers or chopsticks in your hair, or you'll look like you're going to a costume party. Instead, wear it with metallic **strappy sandals** for a night on the town.

LITTLE BLACK DRESS

WHAT IT LOOKS LIKE: The quintessential LBD is simple with clean lines designed to flatter one's best assets. The chesty lady might choose a sweetheart neckline, and a supermodel-tall type may go for a shorter hemline.

WHO MADE IT: Coco Chanel coined the term *little black dress* in 1926 when she debuted her LBD—a long-sleeved, knee-length number with a high neckline. *Vogue* editors may have compared the dress to Ford's Model T (they were both black, sleek, and attainable), but the style far outlasted the 1908 automobile. Though the color choice caused an uproar—black at that point was reserved for those in mourning—the style proved a perfect solution for what to wear to cocktail hour, as it allowed women to sip in style, then easily throw on a wrap or additional layers for dinner on the town. Women today still apply this streamlined dressing philosophy, enabling them to go from work to cocktails to dinner without having to stop home for a change of clothes.

WHO MADE IT HOT: Cartoon character Betty Boop was an early adopter of the LBD ethos. The most famous LBD is the one Holly Golightly wore in 1961's *Breakfast at Tiffany's*. Nowadays, nightlife impresario Amy Sacco (owner of NYC hot spot Bungalow 8) is rarely seen without her LBD.

HOW TO ROCK IT: The genius of the little black dress is that it can be worn for nearly any occasion. It can be gussied up with heels and

Little Black Dress

dramatic jewelry for a trip to the theater or made more casual with a **cardigan** and **slipper flats** for dinner with Grandma. If you can only afford one LBD in your closet, forego glitzy lace or a too-tight-for-church fit; instead, make it simple and versatile enough to work for nearly any occasion.

NEW LOOK STYLE

WHAT IT LOOKS LIKE: This isn't a single dress, but rather a whole style of dressing. Imagine a skirt-top combo that features exaggerated shoulders, a gathered and cinched waistline, and a full skirt to create the ultimate hourglass shape. This style dictated dress shape for a decade after its debut.

WHO MADE IT: Christian Dior first showed this style, dubbed "the New Look" collection, in 1947.

WHO MADE IT HOT: This ultrafeminine silhouetted style came to define the postwar era, thanks to silver screen leading ladies like Audrey Hepburn, Grace Kelly, and Elizabeth Taylor in the late 1940s and '50s.

HOW TO ROCK IT: Anyone who wears this absolutely exudes old-fashioned glamour. Do like Dita Von Teese and wear the cinched, hourglass look with **stockings**, **pumps**, and crimson-painted lips.

New Look Style

Getting Dressed in the Depression

When the New Look was introduced, Americans were still in the throes of an economic depression and appalled at the yardage it took to create its incredibly full, long skirt. Fabric had been rationed in Paris and the US during WWII, and initially most people couldn't afford it. Thus, it took the New Look a whole decade to actually hit the mainstream.

POUF DRESS

WHAT IT LOOKS LIKE: This bouffant **cocktail dress** features a fitted bodice and voluminous layers of silk taffeta that form a wide and puffy short skirt.

WHO MADE IT: In 1986, designer Christian Lacroix introduced this flamboyant creation, which was made from wildly colored and patterned fabrics, like fuschias and rose prints.

WHO MADE IT HOT: Promgoers of the 1980s used and abused the pouf, which they mainly wore strapless. Check out some classic '80s high school flicks like *Sixteen Candles* to see the extravagant pouf in action.

HOW TO ROCK IT: There's no going incognito here. The dress's sheer volume and traditionally loud palatte scream, "Look at me!" If you want to wear the pouf, avoid '80s overkill by choosing simple hair, makeup, and accessories.

Pouf Dress

PRAIRIE DRESS

WHAT IT LOOKS LIKE: Imagine neck-to-toe coverage, dainty floral or calico print, and a ruffled skirt and puffed sleeves. That is the true prairie dress. If that feels too constricting, you'll be happy to know some designers have modified the style, offering more skin-revealing cuts.

WHO MADE IT: This wholesome look dates back to the colonial fashions of the 18th century.

WHO MADE IT HOT: *Little House on the Prairie's* Laura Ingalls helped bring the prairie dress back in the 1970s and '80s. Ralph Lauren sent his style of Americana down the runway with a slightly sexier take on the colonial prairie dress. Fashion renegade Chloë Sevigny has also worn prairie dresses to high-profile events. The look didn't become a huge trend—still, her puritan choices in fashion couldn't have hurt her shot at landing the role of a prairie dress-wearing wife on HBO's *Big Love*.

Prairie Dress

HOW TO ROCK IT: The bad news: Ankle-length cotton dresses don't exactly say "glamour." The good news: They can make a great foundation for DIY reconstruction. Grab a prairie dress from a thrift store and some scissors, and give the dress an updated shape—like a plunging neckline or **midi** hemline—by cutting away some fabric. Then, wear it with something unexpected, like **fishnets** or a studded hoodie.

SACK DRESS

WHAT IT LOOKS LIKE: A waistless, loose-shaped dress that comes to the knee or all the way to the ankle.

WHO MADE IT: Cristóbal Balenciaga introduced the style in 1956. His version narrowed to a point below the knees.

WHO MADE IT HOT: Molly Ringwald constructed a homemade sack dress for her prom in *Pretty in Pink*.

HOW TO ROCK IT: Don a forgiving sack dress with **flat-soled sandals**. Or, for a breezy look, take a sack dress from free-flowing to fabulous by belting it at the waist.

Shattering the Hourglass

The introduction of the sack dress was pretty controversial. Its shapelessness disregarded the Monroe-esqe hourglass figure that was so popular at the time. Some, however, considered the sack a revolutionary choice and even a feminist act: Women were dressing for comfort and practicality, not merely to please men.

Sack Dress

Early Eco-Minded Dressmaking

During WWII, Congress passed laws that rationed the use of fabrics like nylon, which at the time was only to be used to make military gear (such as parachutes for soldiers). Even pockets in clothing were considered an unnecessary extravagance because of the amount of fabric needed. As a result, seamstresses started to use alternative materials to make dresses.

At that time, animal feed sacks were made from cotton and stamped in bright floral, plaid, and paisley patterns. Designing women would hunt for empty sacks of matching patterns (which could be bought for less than a dollar), then use the material to make "feed sack dresses." This endeavor not only earned style points among the community, but also set a recycling precedent for today's eco-minded dressmakers, like Stella McCartney.

Sheath Dress

SHEATH DRESS

WHAT IT LOOKS LIKE: This dress got its name because it resembled a knife sheath—a covering placed on the blade to protect it. The floor-length sheath dress has straight side seams and a slim silhouette.

WHO MADE IT: Some of the first sheaths were dresses worn by Chinese women in the 1600s (see **cheongsam** on page 13). Here in the US, the long, tight-fitting style has come in and out of fashion throughout the 20th century. Oleg Cassini, personal designer to Jackie Kennedy during her White House

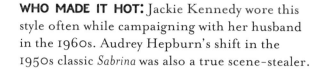

years, created iconic sheath dresses for the first lady in the '60s, inspiring women to go sleek when dressing up for night.

WHO MADE IT HOT: This dress was wildly popular with 1930s film stars like Greta Garbo, who often wore sheaths while demurely waving cigarette holders. Carolyn Bisset wore a simple bias cut, 1930s-inspired sheath as a wedding gown when she married JFK. The sexy sheath she wore launched the career of now-famed designer Narciso Rodriguez who dresses stars such as Sarah Jessica Parker.

HOW TO ROCK IT: The clean lines of the sheath look great with **chandelier earrings** and a pair of **stilettos**.

SHIFT DRESS

WHAT IT LOOKS LIKE: This sleeveless dress with a wide neckline often has darts at the chest, is hemmed at the knee, and can be made to fit tightly like the **sheath** or more loosely in an **A-line** cut. Made using cotton, linen, crepe silks, jersey, or Lycra blends, this style has remained a fashion staple throughout the decades.

WHO MADE IT: The shift became a signature shape for designer Andrés Courrèges in the 1960s.

Shift Dress

WHO MADE IT HOT: Jackie Kennedy wore this style often while campaigning with her husband in the 1960s. Audrey Hepburn's shift in the 1950s classic *Sabrina* was also a true scene-stealer.

HOW TO ROCK IT: Perfectly pair the dress's clean lines and simple elegance with a three-quarter-length coat and heels.

SHIRTDRESS

WHAT IT LOOKS LIKE: This knee-length dress is cut from one piece of cloth, has a front-button closure and collar like an **oxford shirt**, and is usually worn belted at the waist. It's generally made of cotton, rayon, linen, and other wash-and-wear fabrics.

WHO MADE IT: The shirtdress stems from a men's button-up shirt. Its design became part of mainstream fashion in the 1890s and surged in popularity in the 1950s.

Shirtdress

WHO MADE IT HOT: Lucille Ball rocked the hell out of the shirtdress in *I Love Lucy*, but for a more modern take on this style, check out Gwen Stefani's shirtdress in No Doubt's "Don't Speak" video.

HOW TO ROCK IT: The shirtdress is most often worn with pushed-up sleeves and heels.

SLIP DRESS

WHAT IT LOOKS LIKE: Think of the classic slip dress and you think of spaghetti straps, wispy fabrics, bias cuts, and hemlines that hit above the knee, at the floor, or anywhere in between. Featherlight fabrics like chiffon and silk are perfect for keeping this dress slinky and true to its name.

Slip Dress

WHO MADE IT: Minimalist Calvin Klein became king of the slip dress when he sent a young Kate Moss down the runway in one in 1993. Though Madonna was one of the first to wear bras on the outside of her clothes, the success of Calvin Klein's image of waiflike models clothed in scant slip dresses helped solidify the "innerwear as outerwear" trend of the 1990s.

WHO MADE IT HOT: Supermodels Amber Valletta, Claudia Schiffer, Kate Moss, and Naomi Campbell all popularized slip dresses on and off the runway in the '90s.

HOW TO ROCK IT: Layer a solid-colored silk slip dress with a see-through patterned one like Calvin did back in the day.

SMOCK DRESS

WHAT IT LOOKS LIKE: Similar to a painter's smock, this style of dress features smocking (a line of closely pinched fabric) right above the breast line. This tight gathering of fabric high up on the chest encourages the rest of the dress to take on a free-flowing shape.

WHO MADE IT: In the 1970s, the prim and proper Laura Ashley label became famous for selling tons of frilly, floral smock dresses.

WHO MADE IT HOT: Designer Mary Quant dressed Twiggy in a smock dress and **Mary Janes**.

HOW TO ROCK IT: Pair it with opaque **tights** and flats; if you want to go for an old-school artiste look, add a **beret** to the mix.

Smock Dress

Defining Dresses of the Decades

No other garment has reflected the ever-changing ideal body shape for women more than the dress. From the cinch-at-the-waist, hourglass-forming trends of the 1940s and '50s to the waif-friendly slip style of the '90s, the dress continues to dictate which body type is hot at the moment. Which era of dress style best suits your build?

Era	Style	Favored Body Type
1950s	shirt	hourglass
1960s	shift	all
1970s	wrap	curvy
1980s	pouf	slender
1990s	slip	waif

SUNDRESS

WHAT IT LOOKS LIKE: The quintessential sundress features spaghetti or tie-string straps, a puckered bodice, and a full skirt.

WHO MADE IT: The sundress has been a childhood staple throughout American history, but like the **baby-doll dress**, **Mary Jane**, and Peter Pan collar, its style has been co-opted by adults.

WHO MADE IT HOT: Juicy Couture single-handedly put the free-flowing sundress back on the map with its strapless version, worn by Jessica Simpson, Eva Mendez, Eva Longoria, and countless other celebs in the mid-2000s.

HOW TO ROCK IT: This summertime staple looks perfect with a pair of **flip-flops** and a few **bangles**.

Sundress

TANK DRESS

WHAT IT LOOKS LIKE: This dress is like a basic **tank top**, except its hemline extends below the waist. It's typically made of body-hugging fabrics like cotton-spandex blends, and it can be short and supersexy or longer and more elegant.

WHO MADE IT: Knitwear designer Harriet Selwyn's tank dresses were featured in *The New York Times* in 1977, priming the style for its meteoric rise during the next decade's knitwear craze.

WHO MADE IT HOT: Sure, Julia Roberts played a streetwalker in *Pretty Woman* ... but she was a whip-smart, *lovable* streetwalker, making her tiny tank dress one of the most memorable in celluloid history.

HOW TO ROCK IT: This no-fuss dress can be glammed up with a pair of designer **gladiators** or **strappy sandals**. It also makes the perfect poolside cover-up. It generally doesn't have any zippers or other adornments, and can be wadded up and thrown in a beach bag and *still* come out looking like it's been plucked fresh from the closet.

Tank Dress

Skirting a Bearish Market

Do hemlines have anything to do with the stock market? Some researchers say yes. Studies suggest that the higher the hemlines go, the higher the stock prices rise—and as hemlines plummet, so do stocks. Believers of the "hemline indicator" or the "hemline theory" point to the 1920s and '60s as proof. Non-believers contend it's just coincidence.

TENT DRESS

WHAT IT LOOKS LIKE: The tent is an **A-Line** (see page 10) that's cut with excessive amounts of fabric. Laid flat on a surface, the dress looks like a tent.

WHO MADE IT: Cristóbal Balenciaga introduced the shape in 1951 with a coat. He and others then developed dresses in the same form, which later became synonymous with 1960s mod style.

WHO MADE IT HOT: As a regular cast member on *Rowan & Martin's Laugh-In* in the late '60s, Goldie Hawn was the darling of sketch comedy, delivering jokes in short ruffled tent dresses and sex kitten hair.

Tent Dress

HOW TO ROCK IT: The tent is most often paired with flats and **tights** much like its zanier cousin, the **trapeze**.

TRAPEZE DRESS

WHAT IT LOOKS LIKE: The trapeze is an exaggerated take on the **sack dress** that hangs from the shoulders and flares out at the chest. Oftentimes the trapeze is made with enough fabric to hide small children underneath.

WHO MADE IT: Yves Saint Laurent presented the trapeze in his first collection in 1958,

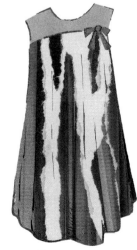

Trapeze Dress

though it would take a few years for the style to infiltrate the mainstream.

WHO MADE IT HOT: Nicole Richie as a girl-about-town in the mid-2000s brought national attention to this style.

HOW TO ROCK IT: The trapeze looks best with simple flats. But beware: This dress could make even the skinniest of girls look pregnant. Try belting the trapeze to give the silhouette a little shape. And remember to wear **tights** or skinny jeans in windy weather—this dress will fly up around your face!

Tube Dress

TUBE DRESS

WHAT IT LOOKS LIKE: The most ubiquitous example of the tube dress is the strapless, form-fitting one worn by Marge Simpson in every episode of *The Simpsons*. The key to the tube dress is its stretchy fabric: Materials like spandex and jersey blends allow the wearer to walk, sit, and breathe without mummylike constriction.

WHO MADE IT: Pierre Cardin showed tube dresses in the mid-'70s, but the style's popularity took off with the unforgivably form-fitting fashions of the '80s. (Hello, spandex!)

WHO MADE IT HOT: Haute couture designer Azzedine Alaia made paint-on tube dresses for supermodels and the superrich in the '80s, but a pre-Beckham Posh Spice brought tube dresses to the masses a decade later by regularly wearing them with sky-high heels. Beth Ditto, the fearless frontwoman of rock band Gossip, has also been known to wear them when she performs.

HOW TO ROCK IT: Tube dresses are great layering tools. Look to American Apparel for inspiration in piling a cotton tube dress with a longer skirt underneath, **leggings**, hoodie, or all of the above.

TUNIC DRESS

WHAT IT LOOKS LIKE: This loose-fitting dress is cut straight from the sides. Traditionally, a tunic's hemline would fall about four inches from the ankles, but many of today's tunic dresses feature above-the-knee hemlines, V-necks, and bold colors. Traditionally made from cotton or silk, like the **caftan**, the tunic is most widely used as a beach cover-up or stylish piece of loungewear.

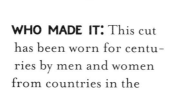
Tunic Dress

WHO MADE IT: This cut has been worn for centuries by men and women from countries in the Middle East, like Turkey and Pakistan. In the early 1900s, designer Paul Poiret made tunic-shaped dresses to cater to women who wanted to dress sans **corset** and to satiate fashionistas' taste for long slender lines.

WHO MADE IT HOT: This is designer and socialite Tory Burch's signature piece. Like Diane von Furstenberg, who built her brand from the wrap, Burch did the same with the tunic in the early 2000s.

HOW TO ROCK IT: The tunic looks best with simple flats or **flat-soled sandals**.

WRAP DRESS

WHAT IT LOOKS LIKE: The wrap is a one-piece, knee-length dress made of cotton jersey. It has a body-clinging cut, and its left and right panels cross in front and are tied together by a built-in sash tie.

WHO MADE IT: Diane von Furstenberg built her fashion dynasty on the wrap she released in 1974. Her marketing slogan, "Feel Like a Woman, Wear a Dress," and her chic and simple design resonated with throngs of American women. By 1976, she had landed on the cover of *Newsweek* magazine, being called "the most marketable woman since Coco Chanel."

WHO MADE IT HOT: The '70s working girl who paired the wrap with a pair of spiked heels inspired legions of followers. Von Furstenberg relaunched the wrap in 1997, and young Hollywood trendsetters, like the Hilton sisters, helped make it hot again.

HOW TO ROCK IT: This is the ultimate travel dress, as the style is extremely versatile (and can easily be dressed up for evening or down for daytime). What's more, jersey doesn't wrinkle.

Wrap Dress

SKIRTS

KILT

WHAT IT LOOKS LIKE: This plaid Scottish wraparound skirt has a flat front and knife pleats that start at the side and follow around the back. It's generally held together on the side with a pin.

WHO MADE IT: Kilts were first worn by Scottish Highlanders in the early 18th century. Back then, four to six yards of woolen plaid fabric were used to make the garment. Wearers would gather the fabric around the waist and belt it to create a pleated effect. Kilts are now ready-to-wear with pleats sewn in.

WHO MADE IT HOT: Famous kilt-wearers include designer Jean Paul Gaultier, Guns N' Roses front man Axl Rose, and Madonna on her Drowned World Tour in 2001. But it was Emma Roberts in the 2007 *Nancy Drew* film who clinched the perfectly preppy look a kilt can bring by pairing hers with penny **loafers** and Peter Pan-collared shirts.

HOW TO ROCK IT: Punk up your kilt like Madonna did by layering it over **leather pants**, or cut your kilt to naughty proportions and wear it with heels for a slightly sexier look.

Kilt

Pleats Defined

accordion pleats ❶ simple single folds in fabric that are narrower at the top and wider at the bottom, made to look like the bellows of an accordion.

box pleat ❷ formed by two folds that meet underneath the fabric, creating a wide pleat on top with inverted pleats between each box. Popular in the 1940s and '50s.

inverted pleat ❸ when two folds of fabric (folded either over or under) meet in the center. This style has been around since the 1920s.

kick pleat ❹ a single pleat placed in the back of a skirt to allow the wearer to walk with a longer stride.

knife pleats ❺ creases just a half to 1-inch apart; all pleats go in the same direction.

Midi-Evil Madness

When designers introduced longer hemlines with the **midi** in the '70s, stores like Bergdorf Goodman uniformed their salesgirls in the look to push midi skirt sales. But the DIY-spirited American chicks of the free-wheeling '60s — who were known to start trends on the street that influenced designers — did not want designers dictating what they should and should not be wearing. Activist groups, like the **miniskirt**-loving GAMS (Girls Against More Skirt) and FADD (Fight Against Dictating Designers) formed to denounce the midi and the designers who pushed the style.

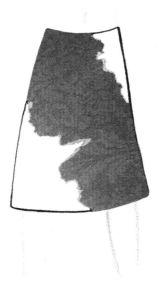

Midi Skirt

MIDI SKIRT

WHAT IT LOOKS LIKE: Any skirt with a hemline that falls at the widest point of the calf.

WHO MADE IT: British designer Ossie Clark introduced the conservative midi in 1967 while **miniskirts** were still at the height of fashion. Three years later, midis began grazing the calves of working women.

WHO MADE IT HOT: Faye Dunaway made the simple midi look absolutely ravishing in the 1967 film *Bonnie and Clyde*.

HOW TO ROCK IT: A skirt that cuts your lower leg right at the widest point can be less than flattering. To avoid the librarian look, choose a midi in a future-forward fabric — like a metallic one. If you do go for tweed, pair it with a slim, silky **blouse**. No matter what type of midi you wear, always pair it with heels to help call attention to slim ankles.

MINISKIRT

WHAT IT LOOKS LIKE: Any skirt more than four inches above the knee is considered a miniskirt.

WHO MADE IT: Designers Mary Quant and André Courrèges have both been credited with inventing the mini. Quant has said she came up with the idea as a child in 1940s Britain after seeing the short skirts worn by tap dancers of the time. Meanwhile, Courrèges first showed his minis in Paris as part of his 1964 collection —about the same time Quant sold her version out of Bazaar, her shop in Chelsea, London.

WHO MADE IT HOT: British legends Vanessa Redgrave, Charlotte Rampling, Twiggy, Marianne Faithfull, and other swinging Chelsea girls of the 1960s all wore minis. By 1969, even shorter versions, called micro-minis, became a favorite among mods.

HOW TO ROCK IT: For a punky look, wear your mini with high-top Converse or **combat boots** like Agyness Deyn. If you're looking to make your mini appear more wholesome, wear it with a long, chunky sweater, opaque **tights**, and **ballerina flats**.

Miniskirt

Pencil Skirt

PENCIL SKIRT

WHAT IT LOOKS LIKE: This **sheath**like skirt is cut in one straight line from the hips to the hem. It's usually made with a single kick pleat in the front or back to make walking easier.

WHO MADE IT: Originally known as the sheath skirt, for its narrow (and fabric-saving) cut, this design came into vogue in the 1940s, when fabric yardage was reduced to help support war efforts. A decade later, it was renamed the pencil skirt after the thin writing instrument, helping paint an image for it as the skirt of the smart, sexy woman.

WHO MADE IT HOT: Joan Crawford was the model of female professionalism with her tight pencil skirts, **blouses**, and broad-shouldered jackets in the noir movies of the '40s and '50s. Alfred Hitchcock, film noir's patron saint, also helped push the look when he famously dressed his stars, like Kim Novak and Tipi Hedren, in smart pencil skirts and towering heels.

HOW TO ROCK IT: Take a cue from Angelina Jolie and pair your pencil skirt with pointy-toed high heels (to elongate the legs) and a simple sweater or capped-sleeved **blouse**.

PLEATED SKIRT

WHAT IT LOOKS LIKE: A skirt made with pleats, or folds of fabric, sewn into the garment.

WHO MADE IT: Pleats have been popular since the 15th century, when royals like Philip the Good of France made pipe-organ pleats (pleats that hang in a series of rolls) popular. In the 19th century, Wattcau drcss plcats (named after painter Jean-Antoine Watteau, who painted women wearing the style) became popular; they ran from the back of the shoulder to the hem of the dress. But the first pleated skirts were **kilts**, which are pleated everywhere but the front panel.

WHO MADE IT HOT: Alicia Silverstone and Stacey Dash in the 1995 film *Clueless* and Selma Blair and Sarah Michelle Gellar in 1999's *Cruel Intentions* all looked perfect in pleats.

HOW TO ROCK IT: Skirts with pleats that start at the waist can make the midsection look wider. Instead, try a style with pleats that start right above the hip. Though pleated skirts almost always conjure up schoolgirl images, put yours with **stiletto boots** and a clingy top for a more sophisticated look.

Pleated Skirt

JEWELRY

Adorning our bodies with sparkling gems and precious metals is nothing new. In primitive times, people wore beads made from seeds, berries, and shells. It's also been documented that, in 30,000 BC, simple pendant necklaces made from bones and animal teeth were popular. And in ancient Egypt, Nubia, and Arabia, pharaohs and queens began wearing gold jewelry in the form of earrings, necklaces, and bracelets. Today we continue the rich tradition—after all, donning a little sparkle is sure to help any girl shine.

CAMEO

Cameos are often made from gemstones that have two layers, like agate and onyx. A carving, typically of a person's head and shoulders, is etched in one layer of the stone so the contrasting color of the other layer is revealed in the background.

Cameos have quite a history. They date as far back as 3100 BC and remained popular throughout the Renaissance and neoclassical periods. When Napoleon gave his wife Joséphine more than 80 cameos at the turn of the 18th century, a fashion trend was born.

Cameos hit their peak in popularity in the Victorian era, appearing on belts, brooches, and bracelets—Queen Victoria and Prince Albert even gave cameo rings carved with the queen's portrait to their wedding guests. Cameron Diaz gave the traditionally serious cameo a cheeky edge when she wore a Hello Kitty cameo necklace to the 2003 Nickelodeon Kids Choice Awards.

Cameo

CHANDELIER EARRINGS

These long, dangly beauties are the queens of drop earrings, typically loaded with sparkling jewels and structured in a garland or triangular tiered fashion, like a chandelier. They became in vogue in the 1920s, when many women wore their hair in short bobs and enjoyed the stunning look of the elaborate jewels against their bare necks. The style has remained popular for formal events throughout the decades. Red carpet superstars like Kate Moss and Nicole Kidman regularly choose chandelier earrings to accent outfits when attending movie premieres and the Academy Awards.

CHOKER

This necklace has also been known as the dog collar because it sits right on the throat. Popular in the 19th century for evening wear—and in the '60s, '70s, and '90s with more casual attire—the choker can be either elegant or tough, depending on its materials. In the '80s and '90s, Princess Diana made quite a statement wearing a multistrand choker of pearls with evening gowns, while punks in the '70s wore chain chokers with padlocks around their necks. Of course, Donna Martin, Brenda Walsh, and Kelly Taylor turned ribbon chokers (especially simple black ribbon ones) into a huge sensation in the early '90s on TV's *Beverly Hills, 90210*.

COCKTAIL RING

Cocktail Ring

As its name implies, this oversize ring with semiprecious or precious stones became popular in the '20s, the era of the cocktail party. Streamlined silhouettes—like those offered by the **little black dress**—called for more dazzling jewelry, and the cocktail ring was the perfect candidate. In the 1941 film *Blood and Sand*, Rita Hayworth was the picture-perfect image of a '40s woman bedazzled in bold cocktail rings, bracelets, and necklaces. Today, red carpet walkers like Cate Blanchett and Sienna Miller wear jaw-dropping cocktail rings although otherwise dressed simply to create an extravagant but not over-the-top look. The cocktail ring was especially prominent at the 2005 Academy Awards; Maggie Gyllenhaal wore one while walking the red carpet and Beyoncé wore one while performing on stage.

Case History

Want to know more about what's behind that glass case at the jeweler's? Here's a rundown of a few more perennial favorites.

bangle bracelet ❷ a firm, thin round bracelet that jangles on the wrist, the bangle has been popular since the 1900s.

charm bracelet ❷ a chain bracelet adorned with different thematic charms of the wearer's choice; for example, a beach fanatic may have a volleyball, surfboard, bikini, and sunscreen on her bracelet.

hoop earrings ❷ this is the oldest type of earring—records indicate they were worn by Sumerian women around 2500 BCE. Nowadays, round-the-way girls cum superstars like Jennifer Lopez are famous for rocking their hoops.

locket necklace ❷ a popular keepsake for centuries, this pendant-style necklace has a locket that opens to reveal pictures of loved ones.

pendant earrings ❷ these drop earrings usually have a single strand of chain and are not as elaborate as chandelier earrings.

pendant necklace ❷ this no-frills necklace features a single charm or gemstone that hangs from the center of a thin chain.

CUFF

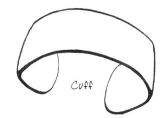

Cuff

This stiff, almost-a-circle bracelet keeps its shape (unless stepped on) and is slipped onto the wrist through an opening on the underside. King Tut wore several cuff-style bracelets at one time around 1300 BC. Wonder Woman, however, must be one of the most famous cuff wearers of all time. With a gold, star-emblazoned cuff on each arm, she stops bullets with her indestructible bracelets and looks fabulous while doing it. But one doesn't need super powers to feel powerful in cuffs—big bracelets are like shields of armor, giving a sense of indestructibility to the wearer.

ID BRACELET

ID Bracelet

This chain bracelet features a small metal plaque, which is personalized with the wearer's name. Servicemen wore ID bracelets fighting in WWII inscribed with their names, ranks, and serial numbers. These men wore the bracelets after they returned home to signify their participation in the war. In 1956, Medic-Alert produced its first batch of medical ID bracelets to help quickly identify those people with diabetes, epilepsy, allergies, and other ailments. While medical IDs are marked with the caduceus symbol (a snake wrapped around a staff), ID bracelets typically bear the wearer's name and may have also been inscribed with a personal message or thought. Jewelry-loving rappers helped bring ID bracelets into fashion in the '90s. Now along with other customized jewelry, like **nameplate necklaces**, consumers can have ID bracelets engraved at most malls.

LARIAT

Similar to a cowboy's lasso, this open-ended long-strand necklace is fastened by looping it into a knot in the front or by stringing it through an O-ring to form a Y shape at the neck. Salma Hayek gave the lariat a boho look in the 2002 film *Frida* by pairing the accessory with rings on every finger and wildly colorful **peasant blouses**. As Reese Witherspoon showed in her 2004 film *Vanity Fair*, lariats can also be elegant. Hers were created by Chanel and made of spar-kling gems. Lariats look best when worn with strapless dresses or anything with a plunging neckline, which pro-vides enough open space to showcase the long style.

Lariat

NAMEPLATE NECKLACE

This chain necklace with scripted text in the center achieved cult status in the late '90s. Though it has been a strong part of street style for decades (New York city kids helped set the trend in the mid-'80s), *Sex and the City* stylist Patricia Field made it a mainstream must-have after dressing the show's leading lady, Sarah Jessica Parker, in a "Carrie" necklace. The piece was so important to Parker's character that she took it with her to Paris in the final episodes of the season, proving to be the one fashion piece that lasted several seasons (and outlasted many, many boyfriends). Never one to miss out on a trend, Madonna's people sent out nameplate necklace invitations to the songstress's "Music" record release party in 2001.

SHOULDER DUSTERS

These extra-long drop earrings draw attention to the neck and shoulders. Edie Sedgwick made her own shoulder-grazing earrings in the '60s, creating a unique style that helped establish her as a fashion icon. In the late '80s, designer Romeo Gigli revived the style when he included it in one of his collections. In the early '90s, supermodel Linda Evangelista pushed the look, appearing in fashion spreads rocking shoulder dusters with her cropped hair.

Sweatbands

STUDS

Short, simple earrings that sit on the earlobe, studs have been worn as far back as 1559–1085 BC. Back then, they were shaped like mushrooms and the "stem" part would be pushed through the ear hole. The stud has evolved (we now have backs for them), but the style is still—and will always be—a favorite. Proper preppy princesses wear pearl or diamond studs; little girls wear heart- and star-shaped studs when first getting their ears pierced; and hip-hop moguls like Sean "Diddy" Combs and Jay-Z wear huge diamond studs on their lobes. Lady-like dressers Kate Bosworth, Reese Witherspoon, Sharon Stone, and Mandy Moore are also known to rock studs in style.

SWEATBANDS

While not technically jewelry, sweatbands are frequently worn as such. Usually made of elastic and terry cloth, these circular, stretchable cuffs fit snugly over the wrists. Though tennis players originally wore them in the '70s (think Luke Wilson as Richie Tenenbaum in the 2001 film *The Royal Tenenbaums*), sweatbands stopped being an athletes-only accessory by the next decade, as the pioneers of hip-hop culture—break dancers, DJs, and MCs—wore sweatbands as a style statement. The trend has continued—clubbers like Lindsay Lohan and DJ Samantha Ronson have been known to rock sweatbands behind the decks and on the street.

TENNIS BRACELET

In the 1920s and '30s, this type of bracelet—a row of diamonds strung together in a straight line—was a popular style, originally known as the "straight line" bracelet. When tennis ace Chris Evert wore one in a televised match in 1987, she caught the attention of tens of thousands of at-home viewers and the style surged in popularity under a new name: the tennis bracelet.

Today's most famous tennis players, such as Anna Kournikova and Serena Williams, keep the tradition alive. Williams even went so far as to borrow a $29,000 tennis bracelet from luxury jeweler Harry Winston for the US Open in 2002. If you think it's too extravagant to wear diamonds with casual tennis duds or everyday jeans and flats (or if you simply can't afford the steep price tag) snag a tennis bracelet made with the more casual and wallet-friendly cubic zirconium.

TOPS AND COATS
Beyond Blouses and Hoodies

TOPS

Today, you've got a lot of choices to make when you get dressed. In addition to worrying about underclothes and overcoats and all their variables, you need at least two basic pieces: something to cover your torso and something to cover your butt. But it wasn't always like that. Before the 1940s, dressing in separates—like combining pants with T-shirts or skirts with sweaters—wasn't frequently done. Many women had a closet full of dresses and that was about it.

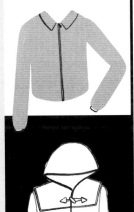

Then, as more women enrolled in college and went to work while their husbands were off fighting in World War II, ensembles that more closely resembled their male counterparts'—like two-piece suits and pants with blouses—came to the fashion forefront.

In fact, the top is now a high-profile element of any woman's wardrobe. And because it is the garment worn closest to the face, a top is often the most memorable part of a person's outfit. Whether we choose a racy halter or classic turtleneck, casual tank or professional twinset, what we wear on top most defines our image.

COATS

Coats are high fashion nowadays, but did you know that most coat styles made their first appearance as military apparel? Your rain-proof multitasking trench coat? First seen on British soldiers in WWII. Your friend's cool-looking bomber jacket? It came straight from the US air force, which designed the garment specifically for pilots. Whether trudging through 35-degree temperatures in Virginia during the Civil War or fighting in a snow-bitten Armenia in January of 1914 during WWI, soldiers have always relied on serious outerwear to get the job done, and designers have always looked to the military for ideas about how to create functional clothing.

Of course, not all coat styles originated from the armed forces. We have Native Americans to thank for the parka. And designer Yves Saint Laurent gave the traditionally manly tuxedo jacket a sultry twist when he created the Le Smoking jacket for women. And some classics, like the trench, aren't even worn as just coats anymore; fashion-forward women tie one on with little to nothing underneath for a night on the town.

Whether you're suiting up to battle the elements or adding a final touch to a feminine outfit, take a moment to really look at—and appreciate—the history and style behind your outermost layer.

CHAPTER GLOSSARY

bodice ❷ the segment of a shirt or coat between the shoulders and the waist.

double-breasted ❷ a style of coat or jacket with two rows of button closures, which overlap a bit in front.

horn-and-toggle closure ❷ a type of closure that fastens by pulling a horn-shaped segment through a wide loop.

lapel ❷ turned-back detail on a jacket, coat, or blouse. The lapel concept originated in the armed forces. When not in battle, soldiers would undo the top button of their high, tight collars and fold the fabric back against their chests. Many of today's suit lapels still feature a buttonhole, as if the jacket had been turned back from a tighter fit.

single-breasted ❷ a style of coat or jacket with one row of button closures.

TOPS

A-SHIRT

WHAT IT LOOKS LIKE: This men's undershirt is a ribbed, traditionally white racer-back **tank** with wide armholes and a slight scoop neck. It's also known as an athletic shirt or a wifebeater (based on the assumption that violent men tend to wear these regularly).

WHO MADE IT: This **tank**, now adopted as outerwear, was born of all-in-one men's underwear called union suits. In the early 1900s, men's underwear evolved into separates, and by the 1930s men were wearing undershirts and boxers.

A-Shirt

WHO MADE IT HOT: Bruce Lee, Kid Rock, and John Travolta are all known for working the A-shirt. In 2002, Shania Twain wore one on the cover of her *Up!* album, and Madonna wore an A-shirt in her "Die Another Day" video, making it a hot item for girls. Madonna was riffing on Marlon Brando's sweaty, dirty, and sexy-in-an-A-shirt look from the 1951 movie *A Streetcar Named Desire*.

HOW TO ROCK IT: Because they're so sheer, these ribbed tanks demand a bra underneath. Pairing your men's undershirt with a hot-pink or black bra adds a little edge to the clean look of white cotton. For a more innocent look, wear it with a flesh-colored **racer-back bra**.

BLOUSE

WHAT IT LOOKS LIKE: Most women's button-up shirts that have a loose waistline or bodice are considered blouses.

WHO MADE IT: Men first wore shirts called blouses in the early 17th century. These were basically loose undershirts meant for absorbing sweat. Blouses made the leap from men's underwear to women's outerwear in the 1860s, when women tried out a more fashionable style called Garibaldi shirts. The full-sleeved, high-necked blouses mimicked the red shirts that Italian military leader Giuseppe Garibaldi chose for his men. This was one of the first instances of women wearing shirts with skirts, though they did so with a rib-cage-clinging belt that made the fit akin to a dress.

WHO MADE IT HOT: Blouses became smart wear with the rise in prominence of working women in the '80s. Some onscreen examples of blouse-wearing leading ladies are Lily Tomlin in 1980's *Nine to Five*, Sigourney Weaver in 1988's *Working Girl*, Elizabeth Perkins in the 1988 film *Big*, and a cross-dressing Dustin Hoffman in *Tootsie* in 1982.

Blouse

HOW TO ROCK IT: Blouses can bring sophistication to anything—even a plain pair of jeans with flats. Because many blouses are made from see-through silks and chiffons, it's good to pair them with **camisoles** for a ultrafemme, but still conservative, look.

CARDIGAN

WHAT IT LOOKS LIKE: A collarless sweater with buttons, snaps, or hooks all the way down the front, a cardigan can be worn open like a jacket or fully closed like a pullover sweater.

WHO MADE IT: The cardigan style came from England's Earl Cardigan, who in 1854 led the Charge of the Light Brigade in the Crimea. Some historians say Cardigan wore his shoulder cape like a button-up jacket. Others contend he wore his long johns top open. Either way, the open-front look caught on and became known as the cardigan.

WHO MADE IT HOT: Grace Kelly was the queen of cardigans with **pencil skirts**.

HOW TO ROCK IT: Whether you wear your cardigan with an old **T**, like Kurt Cobain, or with only the top buttons fastened, like a prim and proper schoolgirl, this lightweight, layer-friendly, and versatile sweater works in all seasons.

Cardigan

CROP TOP

WHAT IT LOOKS LIKE: The waistline of this tiny, tight-fitting **T** or **tank** falls right at the ribs, exposing miles of midriff.

Crop Top

WHO MADE IT: The crop top may have originated, in part, from the *choli*, a fitted half top that Indian women have worn under their saris for centuries. Another midriff-baring precursor to today's crop top is the shirt worn by belly dancers, who first performed stateside at the Chicago World's Fair in 1893.

WHO MADE IT HOT: Barbara Eden in the 1960s sitcom *I Dream of Jeannie*, who wore bra-like crop tops with billowing, gypsy-type pants.

HOW TO ROCK IT: Gwen Stefani layers bikini tops over her crops, further emphasizing her toned abs. But if you don't have the belly to sport this look, try wearing crops like Indian women, as a cool underlayer to other clothing, like **overalls**.

Breaking a Sweat

Sweaters can be knit of a seemingly endless selection of fibers. Here are a few to get you through chilly nights.

alpaca ❶ a material that comes from alpaca, a camel-like South American animal whose fleece makes soft, luxurious fibers for sweaters and outerwear. For anyone with wool sensitivities, alpaca is a great alternative.

angora ❶ supersoft fabric made from the hair of an angora rabbit, often used to make luxury sweaters and scarves. It is more lightweight and doesn't shrink as much as wool. Angora fibers are equipped with air pockets that trap warmth without the weight.

chenille ❶ type of supersoft fuzzy yarn or fabric.

mohair ❶ soft yarn from an angora goat, often used to knit sweaters, mittens, and scarves.

Halter

HALTER

WHAT IT LOOKS LIKE: This top is sleeveless like a **tank** but features a low back. Its U straps wrap or tie around the back of the neck to expose bare shoulders.

WHO MADE IT: The halter neckline was first developed for evening gowns in the 1930s. In 1938, Levi's launched its Katharine Hepburn-inspired Tropical Togs line of colorful denim separates, which included halter tops. The cut went on to become popular for women's beachwear in the 1940s. But it was in the free-wheeling '60s and flashy '70s that halters made out of handkerchiefs and slinky fabrics like Lurex stole the spotlight.

WHO MADE IT HOT: Halston—a designer of slinky gowns worn by celebs to Studio 54 in the '70s—was best known for his sultry halter-style dresses. It was a look carried on by *Sex and the City*'s Samantha, who wore shirts and dresses with halter-top cuts as part of her highbrow, sexed-up character.

HOW TO ROCK IT: Try a high-neck, fitted halter to perfectly juxtapose a pair of slouchy slacks.

Henley

HENLEY

WHAT IT LOOKS LIKE: Henleys are short- or long-sleeved Ts with a slit neckline, no collar, and typically three buttons for closure.

WHO MADE IT: The Henley originated in the mid-19th century as part of the uniforms of the rowing crew in the English city of Henley-on-Thames. Rowers would wear the Henley—then known simply as a **vest**—along with **blazers**, **trousers**, and straw boater hats. These days, rowers wear sporty **tank tops** while on the water, but the Henley still has its place in fashion; it's now a staple of American sportswear, with companies like J. Crew regularly offering it.

WHO MADE IT HOT: Ivy League sporting life-inspired clothiers, like J. Crew and Abercrombie & Fitch, have long borrowed from the rower's uniform, making the Henley popular for decades. Later in her career, supermodel Lauren Hutton wore Henleys for J. Crew in the '90s.

HOW TO ROCK IT: Like a T-shirt, a Henley works with **cords**, jeans, **track pants**—any kind of casual wear. For a layered look, wear it un-buttoned with a cute tank underneath.

Know Your Necklines

boat ❶ a wide neckline that mimics the line of the collarbone.

cowl ❷ a draped neckline that dips down on the chest or across the shoulders.

crew ❸ a neckline with ribbed trim.

keyhole / cutout ❹ a high neckline with a round cutout.

mock ❺ a short turtleneck that stands about 1½ inches tall.

plunging ❻ a superdeep V neckline.

scoop ❼ a U-shaped neckline that dips down on the chest.

slit ❽ a crew neck that creates a narrow V in the front.

square ❾ a wide neckline that drops straight down and crosses horizontally to make a square shape.

sweetheart ❿ a square neck with an M front that resembles the top of a heart.

V ⓫ a neckline that dips down on the chest in a wide V.

OXFORD SHIRT

WHAT IT LOOKS LIKE: Fashioned after a men's work shirt, this shirt has collars that button down and long sleeves with single cuffs.

WHO MADE IT: In 1900, Brooks Brothers introduced the oxford shirt for men. The company emulated a style of shirt worn by English polo players, whose collars were kept buttoned down (and not flying up) while they played. Forty-nine years later, the company finally tailored one for women—made in pink, of course—which helped usher in "prepster cool" among Ivy League American girls and **loafer**-wearing collegiate wannabes.

WHO MADE IT HOT: Candice Bergen has sported oxford shirts both in her private life and in her TV role on *Murphy Brown*, creating a no-nonsense look for the ladies. Scarlett Johansson wore oxford after oxford in the 2003 film *Lost in Translation*.

HOW TO ROCK IT: Take an oxford from straight-laced to saucy by un-fastening the top three buttons and allowing a peek of lacy **camisole** to show through.

Oxford Shirt

Key Collars

butterfly ❷ a wide, oversize open collar with drastically pointy ends.

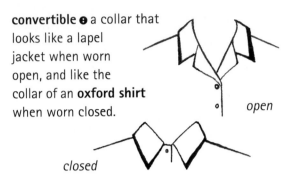

convertible ❷ a collar that looks like a lapel jacket when worn open, and like the collar of an **oxford shirt** when worn closed.

open

closed

Peter Pan ❸ a narrow collar with round ends that fits closely to the neck.

mandarin ❷ a small collar that stands about ½-inch high and sits close to the neck.

PEASANT SHIRT

WHAT IT LOOKS LIKE: This loose-fitting **blouse** can take many forms, but its basic shape lends itself to the **chemise** and it typically has loose-fitting sleeves. It's usually made of cotton or muslin, worn on or off the shoulder, and features a slit neckline or lace-up front.

Peasant Shirt

WHO MADE IT: Male colonial settlers in the 1700s wore peasant shirts, knickers, and long stockings along with their powdered wigs. Though the style originated with European paupers, Yves Saint Laurent created the Rich Peasant and Peasant Chic looks for his 1976 runway shows.

WHO MADE IT HOT: For the ever-cool intellectual Beatniks and folk rockers of the '60s (like Joan Baez), peasant shirts were a wardrobe must. New-school hippie Kate Hudson is the modern-day peasant-shirt fashion plate.

HOW TO ROCK IT: To avoid looking like a full-blown hippie or ren-fair queen, pair your peasant not with a long, flowy skirt, but with tailored, superdark denim and flats or **espadrilles**.

POLO SHIRT

WHAT IT LOOKS LIKE: Essentially a **T-shirt** with a collar, this pullover typically has three buttons at the top center. It can be short- or long-sleeved and is most often made of cotton or cotton pique.

WHO MADE IT: These shirts were originally made of wool and worn for playing polo in the early 1900s. But French tennis player René Lacoste—nicknamed "the crocodile" for his quick game—eventually designed the version known so well today. He first wore his short-sleeved, breathable cotton pique creation on the courts in 1927. In 1933, in one of the first examples of blatant branding, he slapped his crocodile logo on the breast of the shirts and marketed them, creating an iconic style that thrives even today.

WHO MADE IT HOT: Ali McGraw epitomized Ivy League chic in the 1969 film *Goodbye Columbus*. Decked in her white polo shirt, she was *the* rich college girl—a look that was emulated en masse across the country. Gwyneth Paltrow wore Lacoste polo dresses all through the 2001 film *The Royal Tenenbaums*, breathing new life into the old style and brand.

HOW TO ROCK IT: For a preppy look, pop up your collar. For a more modern look, do like Natalie Portman and wear a polo in an unconventional color (like lime green) with a dropped-waist skirt.

Polo Shirt

Writing the Book on Preppy

The term *preppy* was invented by author Erich Segal, who in his novel and movie *Love Story* called a perfectly dressed, perfect-acting person who attended prep school a "preppy." Can't get enough prepster cool? Check out Lisa Birnbach's *The Official Preppy Handbook*, which was published in 1980.

SEE-THROUGH SHIRT
(AKA SHEER SHIRT)

WHAT IT LOOKS LIKE: A top made of chiffon, micromesh, or any sheer fabric.

WHO MADE IT: Though Yves Saint Laurent is sometimes credited with inventing the see-though shirt in 1968, Peggy Moffitt, muse to West Coast designer Rudi Gernreich, wore Gernreich's 1964 version on the streets months before Yves Saint Laurent's Paris show. Gernreich's exposure of the female form didn't stop at the see-through shirt. He was also the first to create the topless bathing suit in 1964—a shocking but successful launch that sold 3,000 suits—and the no-bra bra, a design with sheer netting that simply covered the boobs instead of molding them to a round or missile shape.

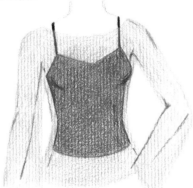

See-Through Shirt
(AKA Sheer Shirt)

WHO MADE IT HOT: Songbirds of every genre have copied Moffitt and Yves Saint Laurent's models. Since the style's debut, rocker Courtney Love, pop star Dannii Minogue, and pop rocker Sheryl Crow have all worn see-through shirts on stage.

HOW TO ROCK IT: It's all what's underneath when donning a see-through shirt. Choose a dark **push-up bra** if you're feeling flashy or a silky **camisole** if you're feeling more demure.

SLEEVELESS SHIRT
(AKA SHELL)

WHAT IT LOOKS LIKE: A sleeveless shirt differs from a **tank top** in that the armholes are cut more narrow and straight, not in toward the shoulder blades. Sleeveless shirts can have a collar or not, be pulled over or buttoned up. A crewneck-style pullover sleeveless shirt is also called a shell.

WHO MADE IT: It's hard to say who created the sleeveless shirt. Like **Bermuda shorts**, it may be that the look was born out of the necessity to keep cool in hot climates. Another theory comes from Australian folklore: In the early 1890s, a sheep shearer named Jacky Howe cut the sleeves off his flannel shirt to help him shear sheep faster than anyone in the world. Some folks still call sleeveless flannels "Jacky Howes."

WHO MADE IT HOT: By wearing **shift dresses** and donning shells for casual shopping trips, Jackie Kennedy and daughter Caroline brought elegance and grace to sleeveless dressing.

HOW TO ROCK IT: Since this is the most conservative style of tank, reserve a sleeveless shirt for visits with the grandparents or a community picnic. By pairing it with a single-strand of pearls or **pendant necklace** and a **pencil skirt**, you'll pass the decency test every time.

Sleeveless Shirt
(AKA Shell)

T-SHIRT

T-Shirt
(Ringer T)

WHAT IT LOOKS LIKE: The T-shirt is cut to resemble the letter T. T-shirts generally have crew necks and short sleeves, though long-sleeved, scoop neck, ringer Ts (shown here), and other styles are also produced.

WHO MADE IT: The T-shirt has naval origins. French, British, and American naval uniforms all included a short-sleeved undershirt in the early 1900s. Legend has it that the British sailors were ordered by captains to sew sleeves onto their undershirts to clean up their look for visiting royals.

WHO MADE IT HOT: Marlon Brando circa 1951 dressed in a plain white T-shirt became the ultimate American tough-guy image—fashion's male counterpart to Marilyn Monroe standing over a breezy street gate in a flowing **halter** dress. In the 1959 film *Breathless*, Jean Seberg was decked in a *New York Herald Tribune* T-shirt, confirming that the look had infiltrated women's wardrobes as well. The University of Michigan was reportedly the first to emblazon T-shirts with a university logo back in 1933. The logo look has since evolved to say a lot about a person: where the wearer has been, what bands they like, and even how they plan to vote.

HOW TO ROCK IT: A T-shirt is the final word in no-fuss style. It has no finicky buttons or fasteners, is made from supercomfortable cotton, and can be paired with just about anything and look fabulous. For the ultimate in effortless style, throw on a T-shirt with a pair of jeans and go.

TANK TOP

WHAT IT LOOKS LIKE: This top has wider arm-holes and thinner straps than the traditional sleeveless top. It's generally fitted and made from wash-and-wear materials like cotton or cotton-Lycra blends.

WHO MADE IT: Before the dawn of the **T-shirt**, men wore tank tops as underwear. The tank didn't become popular in everyday women's dress until skin became a little more "in" during the 1960s and '70s.

WHO MADE IT HOT: Janet Jackson's simple spaghetti-strapped, midriff-baring tank and jeans made a splash when she released her 1990 "Love Will Never Do (Without You)" video, directed by famed fashion photographer Herb Ritts. Of course, her rock-hard abs garnered a little attention, too. Actresses like Franka Potente in the 1998 *Run Lola Run* and Scarlett Johansson in 2007's *The Nanny Diaries* jetted about town in tanks throughout the films, illustrating the tank's sporty side.

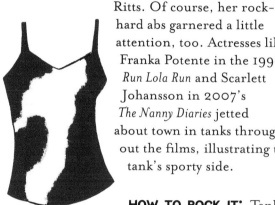

Tank Top

HOW TO ROCK IT: Tanks are another basic that work with just about anything. To jazz up a tank-and-jeans combo, pile on **pendant necklaces** of varying lengths or layer a few tanks so the corresponding straps make the colors of the outer layer tank pop.

THERMAL SHIRT
(AKA LONG JOHNS TOP)

WHAT IT LOOKS LIKE: A long-sleeved crewneck shirt made of waffle-weave cotton, the thermal is a closet staple in winter climates.

WHO MADE IT: Thermals originated in the US in the 1800s when Boston-based boxer John L. Sullivan began wearing long wool underpants as a boxing suit (they became known as long johns). The thin long pants and a matching long-sleeved shirt evolved into flannel and then the waffle-weave cotton people wear today.

WHO MADE IT HOT: In the late 1980s, the grungified rockers of the Northwest may have worn thermals under their flannels out of necessity (its freakin' cold in Seattle), but when their music exploded internationally, the look also exploded and landed on runways in a Marc Jacobs line in the early '90s.

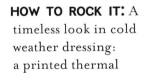

Thermal Shirt
(AKA Long
Johns Top)

HOW TO ROCK IT: A timeless look in cold weather dressing: a printed thermal (anything from hot-pink stars to skull and bones) under a **T-shirt** with jeans.

TUBE TOP

WHAT IT LOOKS LIKE: This tight, strapless top is often held up by an elastic band.

Tube Top

WHO MADE IT: Mosaics that date back to fourth century Greece depicted women wearing tube tops, likely for swimming. Modern-day tubes surfaced in the 1950s, when women paired them with shorts and wore them to the beach. Tube tops are most associated with the anything-goes '70s, when young feminists wore the tube, sans bra, as both a sexy and political statement.

WHO MADE IT HOT: Former *Vogue* editor, jet-setter, and trendsetter Diana Vreeland was regularly photographed in the 1940s and 1950s wearing a tube with high-waisted shorts or a **miniskirt** while on holiday in Southampton. More recent tube-toppers include Chloë Sevigny in the 1998 film *Last Days of Disco* and Cameron Diaz, who wore a rainbow-striped tube to the 2001 MTV Movie Awards.

HOW TO ROCK IT: When worn alone, tube tops radiate the light and breezy sensibilities of summer, but when paired with a light jacket or **cardigan**, the tube can go from tart to tasteful in a snap.

Kashmir Connection

Cashmere fibers come from goats, camels, and yaks raised in the mountains of India, Tibet, Afghanistan, and Mongolia, where cold winters encourage the growth of a soft undercoat of downlike fibers. Until 150 years ago, the processing of these fibers—called *pashm*—into fabric, was done only in Kashmir, India. When the British learned of the Kashmir shawl, they incorrectly referred to it—and the fiber itself—as "cashmere." The name has stuck. Meanwhile, the term *pashm* experienced a rebirth in the West, due to the surging popularity of the pashmina wrap—a silk and pashm scarf that became one of the biggest trends of the '90s thanks to stars like Jennifer Aniston.

TURTLENECK

WHAT IT LOOKS LIKE: A winter must-have, the turtleneck is a pullover that features a high collar that covers the entire neck. When the collar covers only half the neck, the look is called a mock turtleneck.

WHO MADE IT: English polo players first wore turtlenecks in the 1860s. By the early 1900s, the style had become part of US football players' uniforms.

WHO MADE IT HOT: In the 1940s, Greta Garbo and Marlene Dietrich donned turtlenecks with their **trousers**, helping catapult the shirt from sporting uniform to style piece. Audrey Hepburn was famously photographed in her turtleneck, trousers, and flats in the 1950s. The Gap revived this image in their 2006 "Keep It Simple" campaign, showing footage of the late Hepburn dancing in her signature look in the 1957 movie *Funny Face*. And don't forget about Velma, the braniac from *Scooby Doo*, who always wore an orange turtleneck on Scooby adventures.

HOW TO ROCK IT: Turtlenecks will work with pretty much anything—they can take the skin-exposing look of the **mini** down a notch or make **capri pants** look artsy-cool.

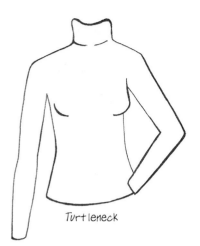

Turtleneck

TWINSET

WHAT IT LOOKS LIKE: A twinset pairs a **sleeve-less shirt** (also called a shell) and a **cardigan** made of the same material.

WHO MADE IT: Coco Chanel created the first twinset in the early 1920s. She used jersey knit cloth—usually reserved for making underwear—to design a crewneck and cardigan from the same color.

WHO MADE IT HOT: Actress Lana Turner sparked a clamoring for sweater sets after she wore them in various films, including 1959's *Imitation of Life*. She became so known for her tight double tops, which she wore a few sizes too small, that she garnered the nickname "the sweater girl."

HOW TO ROCK IT: Twinsets can look a little too "soccer mom" with a simple pair of **trousers**. To funk things up a little, try wearing them with bubble skirts.

Twinset

VEST

WHAT IT LOOKS LIKE: This sleeveless top can be either a pullover sweater vest, usually with a V-neck, or a button-front vest that can be worn with a men's suit, also called a shirtwaist.

Vest

WHO MADE IT: The English adopted the style from the Turks in the 17th century. Rather than creating the vest from silks and muslins as the Turks did, the British used wool to create a gruffer look and made it part of what's now known as the three-piece suit.

WHO MADE IT HOT: Eighties pop queen Debbie Gibson brought the vest out of menswear oblivion and into the closets of thousands of teens. Kate Moss is known as a fashion troubadour, but she is most often photographed in her tiny shorts and open vests worn over **T-shirts**.

HOW TO ROCK IT: A very fitted pinstriped vest (swiped right from a man's suit) looks sexy buttoned up with just a bra underneath.

WHITE CRISP DRESS SHIRT

WHAT IT LOOKS LIKE: This collared shirt with buttons down the front is made of white cotton and often features a breast pocket and single cuffs.

White Crisp
Dress Shirt

WHO MADE IT: Back in the 19th century, the white dress shirt was first worn as formal wear—namely with men's tuxedos. But as Americans moved into the 20th century, the men's dress shirt was chosen for less formal evening events and, finally, the corporate world. It wasn't until the greed-is-good '80s that ambitious, high-powered women began to dress in men's dress shirts when attending both casual and formal functions.

Argyle: From Feet to Geek Chic

The argyle pattern is centuries old, but argyle sweaters and sweater vests are relatively new. Who was responsible for argyle's leap from the socks on Scottish feet to the geek-chic pullovers on our chests? The fashionable Duke of Windsor, who in 1920 asked knitwear specialist Pringle of Scotland to create a sweater to go with his argyle socks.

Pringle fashioned the diagonal segments of tartan plaid in a sweater form—a look that was adopted by Scottish golfers in the 1930s. The argyle wasn't the only sweater the snappy-dressing Duke helped make trendy—when he wore the Fair Isle fisherman's sweater (a pullover sweater knitted with colorful patterns) and the tennis sweater (a V-neck, cable-knit sweater with thick stripes bordering the V) as casual wear, the locals followed suit.

WHO MADE IT HOT: Sharon Stone turned heads by wearing one of her husband's white crisp shirts with a floor-length, **ball gown**-style skirt at the 1998 Academy Awards.

HOW TO ROCK IT: Like the **little black dress**, this classic men's shirt is a wardrobe staple for women. It can be worn with the top buttons undone, or tied at the waist à la '50s glamour queen Marilyn Monroe.

Wrap Shirt

WRAP SHIRT

WHAT IT LOOKS LIKE: Typically
designed with a convertible collar or V-neck, this shirt has one side that wraps on top of the other and ties on the side.

WHO MADE IT: Though the origins of the wrap shirt aren't well documented, this figure-hugging version of the **white crisp dress shirt** likely stemmed from the centuries-old **kimono**.

WHO MADE IT HOT: Ballerinas have traditionally tied thin wrap sweaters over their **leotards** post-workout, giving a chic, sweet, and street look to their dancewear. Company dancers in the 2000 film *Center Stage* tied delicate wraps over their spandex **tanks**.

HOW TO ROCK IT: Even if your best friend is a few sizes smaller than you, the wrap shirt is likely to be the one thing that you can borrow from her closet, since it's very adjustable. Wearing a wrap is a shape-defining move that draws attention to the bust and waist. Wear it with **hip-huggers** or **low-rise jeans** to highlight your assets.

Sleeves and Cuffs

cap sleeve ❶ an abbreviated T-shirt sleeve that barely covers the shoulder.

double cuff ❷ a cuff usually closed with two buttons.

French cuff (aka reversible double cuff) ❸ a type of double cuff that turns back and is fastened with a button.

kimono sleeve ❹ a very exaggerated open sleeve.

knit cuff ❺ a ribbed cuff that provides a tight fit around the wrist.

puff sleeve ❻ this gathered sleeve stands up, away from the shoulder.

single cuff ❼ a cuff usually closed with one button.

three-quarter sleeve ❽ the end of this sleeve reaches the mid-forearm.

COATS

BARN JACKET

WHAT IT LOOKS LIKE: This collared coat is usually lined with fleece. It has a boxlike cut, button closure, and oversize front pockets near the bottom seam.

WHO MADE IT: This look is a riff on the old fishing jackets, called angler jackets, of the 1930s. In the past, the style featured more pockets —on the lower sleeves and breast—for fishermen to hold their gear. Today's barn jackets have the same boxy cut as the angler and still exude the laboring farmhand/fisherman vibe.

Barn Jacket

WHO MADE IT HOT: When Martha Stewart came onto the scene in the '80s, she not only showed Americans how to perfect homemaking, but also spread New England style—including her sensible barn jackets. J. Crew capitalized on the look, offering the style in its catalogs in the '90s and beyond.

HOW TO ROCK IT: This casual overcoat looks great with khakis and a cozy sweater underneath.

BLAZER

WHAT IT LOOKS LIKE: This jacket is similar to the **smoking jacket** in that it has a long lapel and button-front closure.

WHO MADE IT: Blazers became a part of the British navy uniform in 1837, when the captain of the HMS *Blazer* outfitted his crew in spiffy double-breasted jackets for a visit from Queen Victoria. The queen liked them so much, she had other sailors wear the same style. Like with the **pea coat** and, later, **bell-bottoms**, civilians borrowed this naval style. While yachting enthusiasts and collegiate crew team members may not have had the expertise to handle the rough waters like navy men, they could at least dress the part.

WHO MADE IT HOT: Shannon Doherty and Winona Ryder sported blazers at school, afternoon croquet games, and college parties in 1989's *Heathers*.

Blazer

HOW TO ROCK IT: Though blazers can feel a bit pretentious —think college professors and the yachting set—a cropped blazer in a laid-back fabric, like micro-corduroy, looks more relaxed. To complete the ensemble, pair it with **straight-legged jeans** and a flirty **tank**.

Dress for Success

In the 1970s and '80s, as more women joined corporate life, the ethos "dress for success" became pretty popular. During that time, many books came out telling readers that how one presented oneself would dictate how bosses and clients would see them—ideally authoritative, powerful, and impressive. Most popular was John T. Malloy's 1980s *Dress for Success* series, which included a book especially for women on how to dress for the office in "power suits": tailored skirts, jackets with shoulder pads, and conservative jewelry.

BOLERO

WHAT IT LOOKS LIKE: This collar-less jacket is cropped high, near the rib cage. It sometimes has a front tie or button closure, though generally it lies open and flat against the shirt.

Bolero

WHO MADE IT: This type of jacket originated in Spain. For centuries, it's been worn as part of the matador's costume. In the 1940s, re-nowned Spanish-born and Paris-based designer Cristóbal Balenciaga famously incorporated his Spanish roots into his collections by creating intricate boleros for highbrow customers, as did Elsa Schiaparelli, who made a bolero jacket and crepe dress in 1938.

WHO MADE IT HOT: One of Princess Diana's most memorable ensembles was a velvet and ivory satin strapless gown and bolero jacket that she wore to a Paris banquet in 1988. When she auctioned it off in 1997, a year after her divorce from Prince Charles, the dress—which was pictured on the cover of the Christie's auction catalog—earned nearly $100,000 for charity.

HOW TO ROCK IT: Try pairing a beaded bolero with **tuxedo pants** or a **sheath dress** for a fresh take on evening wear.

BOMBER

WHAT IT LOOKS LIKE: This zip-front collared jacket has a puckered waist-band and cuffs. It typically features diagonally cut flat-front pockets.

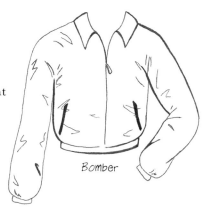

Bomber

WHO MADE IT: The bomber style emerged from the jackets worn by US fighter pilots during WWII. Schott Bros., a New York-based outerwear company, designed a bomber in the 1930s, which the US air force ordered in bulk in WWII. The style has been a part of casual dress ever since.

WHO MADE IT HOT: Kelly McGillis and Tom Cruise inspired bomber mania in 1986 in *Top Gun*.

HOW TO ROCK IT: Bombers look best over a **T-shirt** or **white crisp dress shirt** and **boot-cut jeans**.

Timeless Textiles

Most overcoats come in solid, conservative colors, but here are a few patterns commonly found on classic cover-ups.

chevron stripe ❷ a V-shaped striped pattern similar to the kind found on the Chevron gas station logos.

herringbone ❷ a twill weave that's broken, creating a V-shaped, zigzag pattern.

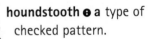
houndstooth ❷ a type of checked pattern.

quilted ❷ a diamond-patterned fabric with filling layers inside.

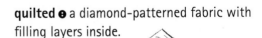

Duffle Coat

DUFFLE COAT

WHAT IT LOOKS LIKE: What makes this heavy, hooded overcoat most recognizable is its horn-and-toggle front closure. It can be made car coat length (hitting the hip) or longer.

WHO MADE IT: The duffle was part of the British Royal Navy's uniform during WWI. By WWII, it became standard issue. After the war, Gloverall, a British outerwear company, purchased the surplus duffles. And when those sold out in 1954, the company began to make its own and continues to be a leading maker of duffle coats today.

WHO MADE IT HOT: Paddington Bear made the duffle world famous. Stars who have taken a cue from the cuddly London icon include Lily Allen and Gwyneth Paltrow.

HOW TO ROCK IT: Pair it with a pleated **midi skirt** like Paltrow in the 2003 film *Sylvia* or layer it over scarves and cozy sweaters for a classic winter look.

MILITARY COAT

WHAT IT LOOKS LIKE: This coat features design elements borrowed from the uniforms of admirals and other military wear. A popular style (shown below) features repetitive horizontal lines flanked with buttons, embroidery, and a button-front closure. Some designs feature a cropped waistline, while others feature a hemline that falls closer to the knee.

WHO MADE IT:
As the name implies, military coats have their roots in military uniforms, with some dating back to the 17th century. Admirals of the day wore decorated knee-length coats—a look that Gwen Stefani's L.A.M.B. clothing label and Juicy Couture make today.

Military Coat

WHO MADE IT HOT: For their 1967 *Sgt. Pepper's Lonely Hearts Club Band* album, the Beatles wore satin military coats in red, chartreuse, blue, and pink that had been rented from a London costume shop. Jimi Hendrix, designer Karl Lagerfeld, and Stefani have also worked the military coat into their clothing lines.

HOW TO ROCK IT: Pay homage to the rock gods by wearing an unbuttoned military coat over a vintage rock **T** and torn jeans.

MOTORCYCLE JACKET

WHAT IT LOOKS LIKE: This leather zip-front jacket has a convertible collar, is cut straight, and has a built-in belt and buckle at the waistline for closure.

WHO MADE IT: Schott Bros. designed its first motorcycle jacket, the Perfecto, in 1928 with the input of bikers and distributed it through Harley-Davidson. But it wasn't until 1948 that biker culture really took off in mainstream America. After fighter pilots and bomber crews came home from WWII, many took to motorcycling to satisfy their need for speed. The leathers they wore to keep warm in the war became an essential second skin while riding.

WHO MADE IT HOT: Marlon Brando was the picture of hellraising biker in the 1953 film *The Wild One*. This look was considered so dangerous that motorcycle jackets were banned from some high schools at the time. Seventies punk princess Nancy Spungen, notorious girlfriend to the Sex Pistols' Sid Vicious, made her motorcycle jacket look even tougher by scrawling political statements on it and stapling studs on the collars and cuffs.

Motorcycle Jacket

HOW TO ROCK IT: One can never go wrong with the trusty combo of jeans, **T-shirt**, and motorcycle jacket, but for something unexpected, try pairing your leather with a strapless, 1950s debutante dress like rock 'n' roll heiress Kelly Osbourne.

NEHRU JACKET

WHAT IT LOOKS LIKE: This single-breasted jacket fits close to the body, has a button front, straight square cut, and 1 ½-inch stand-up collar.

WHO MADE IT: Designer Pierre Cardin returned from a trip to India and immediately dressed his store's salespeople in a gray flannel version of this traditional Indian jacket. In the early 2000s, Nehru jackets were designed for women, as well.

Nehru Jacket

WHO MADE IT HOT: Jawaharlal Nehru, the prime minister of India in the '60s, was shown in *Vogue* magazine wearing this jacket. Soon after, it became known as the "Nehru jacket" and hippies, the Beatles, and Johnny Carson were all wearing one.

HOW TO ROCK IT: The simple cut of the Nehru calls for no-nonsense straight-legged **trousers**.

PARKA

WHAT IT LOOKS LIKE: The parka's length ranges from the waist to the knee. It is a heavy and hooded coat, and typically fur lined or filled with goose down. Some parkas are longer, with a pull cord that ties at the waist.

WHO MADE IT: The word *parka* comes from the 18th-century Russian term for *skin jacket* or *pelt*, but Inuit tribes have worn a sealskin version of this type of coat for centuries. The armed forces also put the parka to good use.

WHO MADE IT HOT: The Olympic skiers in 1932 made mainstream America hot for parkas. More recently, hip-hoppers in the '90s practically made parkas their uniform —Aaliyah, Lil' Kim, and boys of hip-hop Biggie and Tupac all helped popularize bubble goose down parkas produced by companies like The North Face and Tommy Hilfiger.

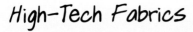
Parka

HOW TO ROCK IT: With hoods and lots of volume, parkas are true coats of armor. They're the perfect coats to make you feel tough and protected at the same time.

High-Tech Fabrics

Gore-Tex ❷ a fabric invented in 1978 that contains a sealant of more than 9 billion tiny holes per square inch, which allows sweat to escape from the fabric while keeping water out.

Kevlar ❷ a strong, lightweight fiber created in the '70s by DuPont, Kevlar was first used in bullet-proof vests, and the material is now used by companies like Levi's and Timberland to create extra-strong jeans and outerwear.

polar fleece ❷ a lightweight, synthetic fiber that traps body heat in while keeping moisture away from the skin. Polar fleece was developed in the early '80s by Patagonia, an outdoor clothier, and came into wide use in the 1990s.

spandex ❷ a man-made stretch material popular in the 1980s and '90s for **leggings**, bike shorts, bodysuits, and **shapewear**.

PEA COAT

WHAT IT LOOKS LIKE:
This double-breasted coat typically has a wide lapel and large front buttons. Its name comes from the Dutch word *pij*, which means a rough, woolen fabric.

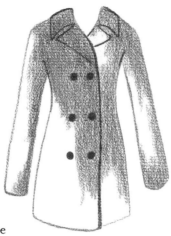

Pea Coat

WHO MADE IT: From the 1830s to WWII in the 1940s, sailors wore this style of coat as part of their uniforms. In 1962, Yves Saint Laurent redesigned the coat with flashy gold buttons for women.

WHO MADE IT HOT: French actress Catherine Deneuve, an Yves Saint Laurent muse, was an early adopter of the designer's pea coat, wearing hers with a striped **shift dress** and flats.

HOW TO ROCK IT: Pea coats look great over **stovepipes**, or slightly longer or same-length **A-line dresses**.

SAFARI JACKET

WHAT IT LOOKS LIKE:
The safari jacket is a belted, lightweight jacket usually made of chino or khaki twill. It features breast and lower front pockets.

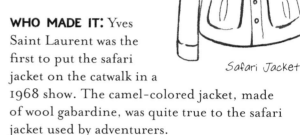

Safari Jacket

WHO MADE IT: Yves Saint Laurent was the first to put the safari jacket on the catwalk in a 1968 show. The camel-colored jacket, made of wool gabardine, was quite true to the safari jacket used by adventurers.

WHO MADE IT HOT: Dressed in a khaki skirt and a safari jacket, Meryl Streep made this style enviably cool in the 1985 film *Out of Africa*.

HOW TO ROCK IT: Simultaneously practical (with big pockets), natural (earth-tone coloring), and dangerous-feeling (the name itself evokes adventure), the safari jacket looks smashing with **trousers** over **riding boots**.

Be-Mused

"Behind every great man is a great woman," the saying goes. And in the art world, you'll find a lot of truth to this. The world's most famous musicians, painters, and fashion designers have long looked to women as muses—beautiful, charismatic beings that inspire the artist to create. In the fashion world, designers depend on women with that certain *je no se qua* to help flesh out ideas for collections, serve as nurturers and encouragers, and while out in public, embody the style the designer creates. After being adopted by an artist, a muse can serve as anything from a collaborator (like Yoko Ono was to John Lennon) to a party companion (like Edie Sedgwick was to Andy Warhol) to a walking billboard (as Isabella Blow was for hat maker Philip Treacy, always wearing his creations about town).

Of course, the notion of muses is nothing new—according to Greek mythology, civilization's original muses were god and goddess Zeus and Mnemosyne's nine daughters, who inspired the master comedians, playwrights, poets, musicians, and astronomers of ancient Greece. Other modern-day muses? Model Loulou de la Falaise to Yves Saint Laurent, singer Vanessa Paradis to Karl Lagerfeld at Chanel, and Audrey Hepburn to Hubert de Givenchy.

SMOKING JACKET
(AKA LE SMOKING)

WHAT IT LOOKS LIKE: Typically made of black silk satin, the smoking jacket is another name for tuxedo jacket ("un smoking" is French for tuxedo). It resembles a suit coat with a long lapel and a two- or three-button closure.

WHO MADE IT: In 1966, Yves Saint Laurent introduced his smoking jacket for women, Le Smoking, as part of a new tuxedo suit he fashioned.

Smoking Jacket (AKA Le Smoking)

WHO MADE IT HOT: In 1975, legendary fashion photographer Helmut Newton shot an image of a model with slicked-back hair donning an Yves Saint Laurent smoking jacket in a Paris back alley. The photo, published in *Harper's Bazaar*, is now legendary—it helped catapult the sexy, powerful image of the androgynous woman and remains one of the most edgy fashion images to date.

HOW TO ROCK IT: For a sleek, sophisticated look, try pairing your smoking jacket with **stovepipes** and **stilettos**.

TRENCH COAT

WHAT IT LOOKS LIKE: This long coat falls right above the knees. It is belted and has a convertible collar, button-front closure, and diagonal-cut front pockets.

WHO MADE IT: Thomas Burberry designed the trench during WWI for British soldiers to wear while fighting … in the trenches. It was double-breasted to keep rain off of the officers' boots and had a wide belt for holding cargo like grenades and a pull-out liner that officers used as a blanket.

WHO MADE IT HOT: Jane Fonda became legendary for her sexy trench and tough-girl shag in the 1971 film *Klute*.

HOW TO ROCK IT: A trench looks great with everything from skinny jeans and **stilettos** to a minidress.

Trench Coat

WINDBREAKER

WHAT IT LOOKS LIKE: This waist-length shell is usually made from water-resistant lightweight fabrics like nylon. It can button up, zip up, or pull over. Its shape is similar to a **bomber**, but it hangs straight instead of hugging the waist.

WHO MADE IT: This jacket was molded after the waterproof British Royal Air Force flying jackets in the late 1940s. In England, it's also called a windcheater.

WHO MADE IT HOT: Windbreakers have been a popular part of hip-hop fashion since the '80s. Lady rhymesayers Monie Love and J.J. Fad helped launch the trend, and Missy Elliot has kept it going.

HOW TO ROCK IT: Because nylon can puff out a lot, windbreakers work well with baggy jeans.

Windbreaker

Fluffed-Up Fonz

When ABC reviewed the first footage of the TV show *Happy Days*, executives saw the Fonz's leather jacket as something indicative of "criminal, violent, and homosexual behavior." To keep the show squeaky clean, they changed his jacket to a light-blue **windbreaker**. Eventually, producers persuaded the studio to approve of the tougher, leather-clad Fonz.

HATS

Celebrities and hats have shared quite a connection over the past century. It started in the golden age of cinema, when high-profile stars like Marlene Dietrich, Greta Garbo, and Humphrey Bogart wore **fedoras** and **cloches** to help establish an onscreen mysteriousness, and starstruck viewers followed suit. As the decades passed and fewer film characters were costumed in complete hat-glove-shoe ensembles, Americans also went hatless. By the '80s, ultracasual style ruled both the screen and the street, and **baseball hats** stole the favor of celebrities and pedestrians alike.

In recent years, celebrities—desperate to escape the paparazzi and our obsessive star gazing—have begun wearing baseball caps and other brimmed hats as a way to travel incognito. The public, always quick to emulate celebrity style, is in on the action. Today, actresses, rappers, and imitating youth don everything from crushers to **military caps** as part of their street style.

BASEBALL HAT

This billed cap with a dome-shaped crown is sometimes constructed with an adjustable band or elastic in back for a customized fit. The hat obviously got its name from the sport of baseball, but it didn't originally have a shade-creating bill. The bill-less kind was first worn around 1860, and the hat underwent its design change decades later in the early 1900s. In the 1920s, the billed-style hat became popular among the masses, as fans emulated their favorite players like superstar Babe Ruth. Truck drivers also adopted the style, wearing hats with a padded front and nylon net in the back for coolness. Actor Ashton Kutcher helped bring back the trucker hat when his TV show *Punk'd* debuted in 2003. Soon after, everyone from Madonna to Hilary Duff hopped on board the trucker hat bandwagon.

Beanie

BEANIE

These brimless knitted hats hug the skull. Historians say that Lewis of Lewis and Clark wore a beanie while on his famous expeditions. Cricket players at Princeton and Yale wore knitted skullies in the late 1870s when playing matches. By the 1930s, these hats were called calots and were worn set back on the head in an abbreviated version of the modern-day beanie that stopped just above the ears. In the '60s and '70s, surfers, skiers, and skateboarders claimed the look as part of their street-inspired sportswear. It's remained popular with snowboarders, like Barrett Christy and other extreme sports fans and participants.

BERET

You may think of the beret as the quintessential headgear of French painters parading around Montmartre, but it actually has its roots in the military. In fact, it's the most common military hat in the world. In the 1930s and '40s, during cinema's golden age, Hollywood legends like Lauren Bacall, Greta Garbo, and Bette Davis helped take the felt beret from a military standard to a sophisticated ware. The beret became a symbol of female mystique, as these leading ladies strutted them on and off the set, peering out from the one eye not shaded by the cocked-sideways brim. Ultimately, Faye Dunaway, as gun-toting vixen Bonnie Parker in the 1967 film *Bonnie and Clyde*, inspired the masses to hunt for Depression-era berets and tight sweaters, mirroring her famed attire in the movie. Fashion publication *Women's Wear Daily* labeled the phenomenon "the Bonnie and Clyde syndrome."

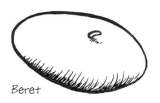
Beret

BUCKET HAT (AKA FISHER-MAN'S OR CRUSHER HAT)

This hat has a round, flat top and a small brim and is typically made of soft fabric. The bucket was first introduced around 1900. The most famous bucket hat wearer? Gilligan from the 1964 TV show *Gilligan's Island*. While the style has consistently been a favorite of fishermen and the J. Crew set, hip-hoppers gave it a new spin in the '80s. Led by a baby-faced LL Cool J, who wore a Kangol bucket hat on the cover of his *Radio* album in 1984, the street-started trend inspired luxury fashion houses Burberry, Gucci, and Chanel to make their own logo-emblazoned bucket hats. Of course, Kangol still remains synonymous with hip-hop street style, thanks to LL, Samuel L. Jackson, and others with a strong allegiance to the brand.

CLOCHE

This old-school hat was the most popular women's headwear of the 1920s. It fits snug on the head, has a soft, short flexible rim, covers from the back of the neck, and is worn pulled down over the forehead. A cloche can be brimmed or brimless and is sometimes decorated with grosgrain ribbon. The cloche was to Greta Garbo what the bowler was to Charlie Chaplin, and Garbo quickly became the poster child for the style in the '20s and '30s. Stars seeking old-world glamour still bring out this classic hat from time to time; Sienna Miller was photographed for the cover of *Life* magazine donning a cloche in the February 2007 issue.

COWBOY HAT

This wide-brimmed hat, often worn purposefully tattered and beaten up, is the quintessential American dome piece. One of the original cowboy hats, the Stetson, was invented by John B. Stetson in the 1860s to help shade cowboys' faces from the sun while on horseback. The classic cowboy hat has been worn by cowboys, like Buffalo Bill and Roy Rogers, and by presidents Dwight Eisenhower, Lyndon B. Johnson, and Ronald Reagan. The cowboy hat hit runways in the mid-'80s when Vivian Westwood created a version for her Buffalo Collection. Present-day country lovers like Jewel keep the cowgirl tradition alive.

FEDORA

A narrow-brimmed hat with a pinched front and crease in the crown, the fedora was named after an 1882 French play called *Fédora* in which the lead character (Fédora) wore this type of hat. Though it was a woman who introduced the fedora, the hat has historically been more of a guy thing, worn excessively by the newsmen of the 1940s (who would carry their press passes in the bands of their hats) and screen legends like Humphrey Bogart, for whom the fedora was a signature accessory. However, women have been tapping into the fashion in recent years; today's style mavens like Cameron Diaz have been seen in fedoras, giving the classic hat a feminine touch.

Fedora

MILITARY CAP
(AKA FATIGUE HAT
OR LEGION HAT)

This cap kind of looks like a **baseball hat**, but it has a square, rather than round, structure on the front crown. This style was modeled after German forage caps worn in WWII and became popular for everyday use in the '60s. Celebrities like Fergie and Jessica Simpson who want to turn up the style volume but still go incognito don military caps and shades while shopping on Robertson Boulevard or eating at The Ivy.

Military Cap
(AKA Fatigue Hat
or Legion Hat)

NEWSBOY

This round hat that snaps down on the brim was popular among paperboys of the 1920s and was made iconic by Jackie Coogan, a child actor in 1920s silent films. Later, Edie Sedgwick made it chic and an absolute must-have for the young, hip crowd of London's Carnaby Street in the '60s. More recently, in the 2006 film *The Devil Wears Prada*, Anne Hathaway as Andy Sachs donned a newsboy after her fashion makeover.

Newsboy

PORKPIE HAT

This style of round hat—with its snap brim and crease on the edge of the crown—may have reached its peak of popularity in the 1930s and '40s, but it's continued to be a favorite of musicians. Jazz musicians like Count Basie popularized the style in the '50s. In 1959, Charles Mingus composed a tune, "Goodbye Porkpie Hat," a song about jazz great Lester Young, who was known for wearing this style. A decade later, ska musicians picked up the look, wearing them with pencil-thin ties and suits. Debbie Gibson wore one on the cover of her 1989 album, *Electric Youth*. Then, after more than a decade in obscurity, the porkpie hat was resurrected by popstar Fergie when she started wearing them around 2005.

SUN HAT

The wide-brimmed sun hat evokes an image of a Southern belle mingling at a garden party. It started as a boater hat, a circular straw hat with a flat top and straight brim worn by boaters from the 19th century until the 1940s. Shortly afterward, the bigger, floppier sun hat came into style and remained popular for decades. It became a celluloid fave in the 1990 film *Pretty Woman*, when Julia Roberts wore a dignified sun hat to a polo match. Stars like Vanessa Minnillo, Gabrielle Union, and Star Jones all wore fancy sun hats at the 2007 Kentucky Derby, taking part in a decades-long tradition for attendees of the event.

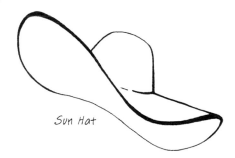
Sun Hat

VISOR

First made fashionable by tennis players in the mid-1920s, visors—essentially **baseball hats** with the crown lopped off—have become fashion staples for many youth tribes, including hip-hoppers, ravers, and the Abercrombie & Fitch set. Actress and golfer Catherine Zeta-Jones has worn visors on the course, keeping the style's preppy roots in check, and funnyman Jamie Kennedy donned a backwards visor in the 2003 movie *Malibu's Most Wanted* while playing a white kid trying to emulate black culture.

Hat Head Help

The downside of wearing something on your head? Unsightly hat head. Here are some tips for avoiding frizzy or super-flat hair:

❶ Make sure your hair is completely dry before putting on a hat—the moisture left in wet hair will act as a sealant and leave your hair to dry smashed against your head.

❷ Use a little bit of styling spray before you put on a hat to help hold your hair's pre-hat volume.

❸ Once you remove your hat, flip your head upside down and run your fingers through the roots of your tresses to wake them up.

❹ Reduce static and frizzies by rubbing the inside of your hatband with a sheet of fabric softener.

❺ Use conditioner. Dry hair is more prone to post-hat flyaways, but moisturized hair topped with a shine serum will stay in place.

PANTS AND SHORTS
Dressing for Power and Play

The average American owns nine pairs of jeans—more denim per citizen than in any other country. But our love for denim goes deeper than casual comfort. Pants represent two very American qualities—power and freedom. It's even in our language: When we say, "Who wears the pants in the relationship?" we're really asking, "Who calls the shots?" And the phrase "too big for your britches" indicates that you're acting more important than your pants size—or status—deems appropriate.

Then there's the practical freedom that pants provide. We can exercise a full range of movement when wearing trousers, unlike when we are bound by a **sheath** or **tube dress**, and can do everything from scale trees to ride motorcycles to jump hurdles.

Of course, it wasn't always like this; women were restricted to skirts and dresses until just a couple of hundred years ago when a few fashion-forward femmes took the reins. Back in the 1800s, when Victorian dress dictated women's wear, renegade homesteaders and cowgirls like Calamity Jane were among the first to defy the dress code. When the women of the 1940s took over the day jobs of the men who left to fight in WWII, they had to wear pants as part of their new uniforms (like conductors suits and doctors scrubs) to give them the freedom they needed to get the job done. Coverall-clad Rosie the Riveter, the fictional woman who represented the female working force of the '40s when she flexed her bicep and declared "We can do it!" all over national billboards, became an American icon.

This can-do attitude and newfound power in the workplace carried over to Hollywood, where a few standout stars showed that the pants craze wasn't just about working—it was about sex appeal, too. Screen goddesses Marlene Dietrich and Katharine Hepburn showed the world that women could be sexy when sporting menswear by wearing it themselves in movies like *Morocco* (1930) and in everyday dress.

As the years went on, and women's lib hit full throttle, pants eventually became a staple of every female's wardrobe. Now, when we step into our cargos, trousers, or yoga pants we're not only allowing ourselves the freedom to dance, run for the bus, or play up androgyny, we're flexing our power as athletes, professionals, and hard-core hobbyists. In our pants, we're continuing to break down walls in sports, boardrooms, and daily life—and actualize our potential as kick-butt human beings.

CHAPTER GLOSSARY

flaring ❷ gradual widening near the end of the garment.

tapering ❷ gradual narrowing of fabric.

rise ❷ the length of fabric from the crotch to the waistline.

PANTS

BELL-BOTTOMS (AKA FLARES)

WHAT THEY LOOK LIKE: Bell-bottom pants flare out to a bell shape at your feet.

WHO MADE THEM: This style emerged from the uniforms of sailors. Back in the 15th century, Italian and Indian sailors wore wide-legged pants made of cotton, linen, or wool because the style was easy to roll up when the decks got wet and easy to pull off over shoes if a sailor fell overboard. The US Navy opted for this design as well and only discontinued issuing bell-bottomed uniforms in 1998, when it went with a more modern, straight-legged design.

WHO MADE THEM HOT: In the 1960s hippie scene, both men and women wore bell-bottoms with patterned shirts and fringed **vests**. While the look was popular, it wasn't until the '70s that bell-bottoms earned their disco-dud reputation after being worn by divas Cher and Diana Ross.

HOW TO ROCK THEM: Reviving bell-bottoms can be tricky. (It's easy to look like a leftover extra from *Saturday Night Fever* or *That '70s Show*.) Most of today's bell-bottoms are called flares and are cut more narrowly. To avoid fashion failure, try wearing flares as part of a more streamlined look, either with a toned-down top in muted colors or, like Kate Moss, with a simple **leotard**.

Bell-Bottoms (AKA Flares)

Hilfiger's Hippie Roots

Tommy Hilfiger's fashion empire got its start with seed money he earned in 1969 from selling bell-bottoms that he and a friend bought in New York City and then sold to folks in his fashion-starved hometown of Elmira, New York. The duo used the profits to launch its first hippie-inspired clothing store, called People's Place. Later, some of Hilfiger's first fashion designs included sketches of bell-bottoms and jeans.

BOOT-CUT JEANS

WHAT THEY LOOK LIKE: These jeans flare out a bit at the leg and have wide belt loops.

WHO MADE THEM: Wrangler released one of the first boot cut styles, the "cowboy cut," in 1947. The higher pockets kept cowboys' wallets from falling out while on horseback, wider belt loops helped accommodate their big-buckled belts, and slightly flared legs provided enough room to cover their **cowboy boots**.

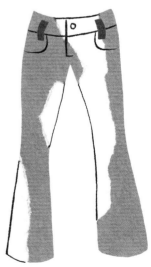

Boot-Cut Jeans

WHO MADE THEM HOT: The 1991 film *Thelma & Louise* was all about the butt-hugging boot cut. Well, and a young, hot, shirtless Brad Pitt (sigh). Pop singer Jewel is also known for her boot-cut jeans and big-buckled belts.

HOW TO ROCK THEM: Unlike other styles of jeans, boot cuts look great on all body types. It's best to wear them with bulkier shoes or, as the name suggests, over boots.

BOYFRIEND JEANS

WHAT THEY LOOK LIKE:
These straight-legged jeans fit relaxed around the bum and thighs.

WHO MADE THEM:
Back in the day, a girl had to nick her man's jeans to rock denim, which meant that her pants were usually too big—but supercomfy. Manufacturers finally began mass-producing jeans for women in the '70s and called the roomy, straight cut the "boyfriend cut" (finally, with no boyfriend necessary).

Boyfriend Jeans

WHO MADE THEM HOT: Jean-stealing girl-friends of the '50s and '60s, like the tomboyish Jan in *Grease*, brought attention to this style. Gwen Stefani takes boyfriend jeans a step further in the borrowing-from-the-boys department—she wears hers over **boxers**.

HOW TO ROCK THEM: These easygoing blues look best worn faded and dressed down, with classic kicks, like slip-on Vans, and your favorite **T-shirt**.

BREECHES (AKA JODHPURS OR RIDING PANTS)

WHAT THEY LOOK LIKE: Most breeches fit like **leggings** and taper right down to the ankles. They are a lot like 1980s-style stretch pants, but made with thicker, more rugged fabrics, like heavyweight nylon.

WHO MADE THEM: Breeches became a popular style for casual men's dress in the early 1800s and were then called pantaloons. In the late 19th century, women began wearing jodhpurs, a variation of breeches that came from Jodhpur, India, and were used for riding horses. Jodhpurs traditionally balloon from the hip to the knee and taper from the knee to the ankle, with stirrups under each foot, though current styles resemble the tight fit of breeches.

WHO MADE THEM HOT: Athina Onassis, an equestrian competitor and granddaughter of Aristotle Onassis (Jackie Kennedy's second husband), brought an international spotlight to riding chic. Princess Diana and Paris Hilton have also been photographed in breeches.

HOW TO ROCK THEM:
When it comes to riding pants, the best looks are classic. Pair them with a thick, oversized sweater and knee-high **riding boots** that slide over the pants.

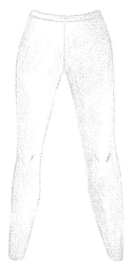

Breeches (AKA Jodhpurs or Riding Pants)

CAPRI PANTS

WHAT THEY LOOK LIKE: This cropped pant has a flat front, figure-hugging cut, and a hemline a few inches below the knee. They're shorter than **clam diggers** but slightly longer than **pedal pushers**.

Capri Pants

WHO MADE THEM: In 1949, while Emilio Pucci was on vacation in Capri, Italy, he dreamed up his famous capri pant, giving jet-setters an alternative to **New Look**-style skirts.

WHO MADE THEM HOT: Long before *Sabrina, The Teenage Witch* TV show, there was *Sabrina*, the movie. The 1954 film starred style legend Audrey Hepburn, who famously wore capri pants, **ballerina flats**, and a long-sleeved top—all in black. Mary Tyler Moore also fed the capri craze by wearing them on *The Dick Van Dyke Show* in the '60s.

HOW TO ROCK THEM: Capri pants evoke the spirit of summer, vacationing, and the beach, so keep the look simple by pairing the pants with flats and a **halter top** or collared **sleeveless shirt**.

CARGO PANTS

WHAT THEY LOOK LIKE: Most casual cargo pants are fashioned after the ones worn by the military, with features like drawstrings, oversize pockets, and a reinforced seat. Cargo pants have been reinvented in just about every fabric and length. Designers have whipped up silk, satin, linen, and denim versions adorned with embroidery, side ribbons, and hardware, making these traditionally rugged pants very versatile. The cargo's greatest perk? With enough pocket room for *your* artillery—phone, keys, lip gloss, wallet, and even a bottle of water—they pull double duty, serving as a purse replacement, too.

WHO MADE THEM: The first cargos were part of the British army's uniform in 1938. The American forces got their version a few years later as the country prepared to fight in WWII. The signature oversize side pockets were first designed as an inverted box, then modified with accordion pleats to better carry ammunition and free up soldiers' hands.

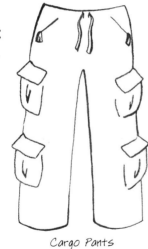

WHO MADE THEM HOT: Cargos have been in and out of fashion since they became popular in the '60s. The modern-day cargo queen is Fergie, who wears them when she's not glamming it up onstage.

Cargo Pants

HOW TO ROCK THEM: Cropped satin cargos demand **strappy sandals**, while old-school camo styles look best with **flip-flops**.

CHINOS

WHAT THEY LOOK LIKE: The term *chino* actually refers to a fabric, not a style. Chino is a khaki-dyed cotton fabric with tiny textured diagonal lines, or twill. Chino pants can be classified as any long pant—either a flat-front or pleat-front **trouser**—that is made with this type of fabric.

WHO MADE THEM: Sir Harry Lumsden invented chino fabric around 1846 when he was completing military service in the Middle East in Peshawar. He dressed his regiment in durable cotton twill that was dyed the color of the sandy desert using a mixture of coffee, curry, and mulberry juice. Though this is now considered one of the first camouflage uniforms, Lumsden wasn't actually motivated by any covert operation; he reasoned that using a dye so like the color of sand would keep his soldiers' uniforms looking cleaner than they actually were. So, how did chinos get their name? In the late 19th century, English textile producers began to ship khaki cloth to the British army in India, which sold the surplus material on to China, who then sold it to American forces. Thinking the cloth originally came from China, the Americans dubbed it "chino."

Chinos

WHO MADE THEM HOT: American soldiers based in the Pacific were issued chino pants in WWII as part of their uniform. After the war, soldiers continued to wear the comfortable pants as casual wear, giving denim a run for its money. Now, companies like Dickies are known specifically for their chinos. Reese Witherspoon's character in the 1996 film *Freeway* rocked Dickies as did Fergie in her "Glamorous" video. They were both emulating the gangster-fab garb popularized by cholas in LA.

HOW TO ROCK THEM: Chinos can look preppy (like Dockers) or street-savvy (like Dickies) depending on the style, but each has a distinct look. If your pants are J. Crew, pull out the **loafers**. If they're street, cop the Converse.

CIGARETTE PANTS

WHAT THEY LOOK LIKE: The hemline of these slim-lined, tapered pants falls right above the ankle. They're often made of stiff silks and sit right at the natural waistline.

WHO MADE THEM: Cigarette pants became popular in the 1950s when original desperate housewives donned these skinny pants in efforts to emulate Alfred Hitchcock's leading ladies. A decade later, designer Pierre Cardin created cigarette pants for men, and the skinny cut became uniform for bands like the Rolling Stones.

WHO MADE THEM HOT: Designer Kate Spade is so known for her love of cigarette pants that in 2004, Mattel introduced a limited edition Barbie by Kate Spade, dressed just like the designer in a floral print coat with cropped sleeves, ivory sweater, and green silk cigarette pants.

HOW TO ROCK THEM: The cigarette pant paints a skinny line, so be sure to pair it with something form-fitting up top, like a thin sweater and slipper-style flats.

Cigarette Pants

CLAM DIGGERS

WHAT THEY LOOK LIKE: These fitted pants stop at the calf and are traditionally high-waisted. They're often made of light cotton, seersucker, or twill.

Clam Diggers

WHO MADE THEM: At first, clam diggers were considered to be any pair of sawed-off blue jeans that people wore while wading in the ocean (while looking for clams). In the 1950s, the look and length of the pant became popular with the nascent surfer culture.

WHO MADE THEM HOT: On screen, Sandra Dee (the original Gidget) and Annette Funicello brought clam diggers to the beach as a cover-up for their itty-bitty bikini bottoms.

HOW TO ROCK THEM: Like with **capris** and **pedal pushers**, clam diggers look best with simple **sneakers** (like Keds) or flats and a **henley**.

CORDUROYS

WHAT THEY LOOK LIKE: These pants are similar to jeans in their cut and style but are made from a durable cotton fabric that's ribbed like a cord or rope.

WHO MADE THEM: The term *corduroy* came from the French *cord du roi*, meaning "cord of the

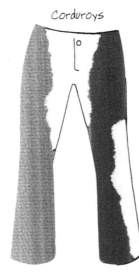
Corduroys

king." In the 1700s, pants that were called corduroys were silk and used to clothe the king's servants. By the late 1800s, this style of pants ended up stateside, in Providence, Rhode Island, where manufacturers switched silk for durable cotton. This new type of corduroy even made its way into the driver's seat—Henry Ford upholstered the interior of his 1918 Model T with the popular fabric.

WHO MADE THEM HOT: Nearly every fashion megastar has been photographed in cords: Mia Farrow wore wide-set cords with a heavy sweater in the 1968 film *A Dandy in Aspic*, Princess Diana was photographed with hers tucked into **Wellington boots** circa 1981, and Missy Elliot and Madonna rocked blue cords adorned with studs and the letter M stitched on the pockets in a 2003 Gap ad.

HOW TO ROCK THEM: Cords are as durable and comfy as your favorite pair of jeans. The best way to wear them? Throw on a **peasant shirt** and call it a day.

Fabric Fundamentals

stretch ❷ a term used to describe fabric infused with Lycra to give a stiff fabric, like denim, some flexibility.

tweed ❷ this is a popular weaved wool used for **trousers** and overcoats alike. It was developed in Scotland in the early 19th century.

velour ❷ *velours* is French for velvet. Both velour and velvet are woven with the same process of looping threads. Velour is made from cotton as opposed to velvet, which is made of silk.

CULOTTES

WHAT THEY LOOK LIKE: Culottes look like a full skirt but are divided like pants. The pant legs are cut wide to create a skirtlike image of one piece of cloth when the wearer is standing still. Lengths vary from calf to ankle. Mid-calf lengths are also called gauchos, a style that was taken from South American cowboys and became popular in the 1960s and '70s.

WHO MADE THEM: In the early 1800s, culottes and tight-fitting knee **breeches** (which looked a bit like white biker shorts) were worn only by elite Frenchmen. Meanwhile, the revolutionaries who stormed the Bastille in 1789 wore rough-and-tumble trousers instead and became known as "sans-culottes." Famed French designer Paul Poiret introduced culottes for women in 1927.

Culottes

WHO MADE THEM HOT: Fashion daredevil Cher brought the style to a whole new level when she wore a Bob Mackie turquoise culottes-and-top ensemble peppered with mirrors and ostrich feathers. Culottes have also seen a lot of action in the sports world. Before jogging shorts and **sports bras** were common garb, culottes reigned as women's sportswear. Hunting Frenchwomen wore them under their skirts and American cowgirls donned culottes to avoid sidesaddle-in-a-skirt restrictions. In 1931, designer Elsa Schiaparelli created culottes for Wimbledon player Lily d'Alvarez to wear on the courts (they controversially showed a bit of thigh). And in the 1990s, tennis ace Jennifer Capriati also wore culottes at Wimbledon.

HOW TO ROCK THEM: In winter, tweed culottes that fall to mid-calf look great with a chunky sweater and **stiletto boots**. Cotton-Lycra culottes and spaghetti-strap **tanks** make perfect summer travel wear.

DRAWSTRING PANTS

WHAT THEY LOOK LIKE: These roomy, often straight-legged pants feature a string or ribbon embedded in the waistband to cinch for a perfect fit.

WHO MADE THEM: Drawstring pants were introduced as unisex pants in the '60s. Though no one noteworthy dreamed them up, most likely the design was an offshoot of men's military combat pants.

WHO MADE THEM HOT: The women of TV's most famous medical dramas—from Loretta Swit on the '70s show *M*A*S*H* to Julianna Margulies on the '90s episodes of *ER* to Ellen Pompeo on the 2000s show *Grey's Anatomy*—all took the look of drawstring pants from so-so to smokin'.

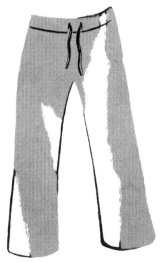

Drawstring Pants

HOW TO ROCK THEM: Because these pants pull off and on, they're an easy choice for lounging, boating, and beachwear. Linen drawstring pants look great with a simple black **T-shirt**.

HIP-HUGGERS

WHAT THEY LOOK LIKE: Hip-huggers are cut low and tight in the seat and thighs and traditionally flare out down the leg.

WHO MADE THEM: Fred Segal (of the famous Fred Segal Boutique in Santa Monica, California) started his fashion business in 1960. A sportswear salesman at the time, Segal saw a market for hip-hugging denim. But when he pitched the idea to his bosses, they laughed him out of the room. Segal set out on his own, making his signature pants in velvet, velour, leather, mohair, and thick corduroy.

WHO MADE THEM HOT: Segal's pants became fast favorites of Jim Morrison and Elvis Presley. And when Warren Beatty starred as a playboy in the 1975 movie *Shampoo*, he wore Segal-inspired hip-huggers to show off his manhood. In the late '90s, Jennifer Lopez almost single-handedly brought hip-huggers back from the brink. She's worn them on stage and in videos, and wore them with a **crop top** and bandana tied around her forehead at the 2000 MTV Music Video Awards.

HOW TO ROCK THEM: Hip-huggers look cute with a **wrap shirt**. But remember, no matter how modestly you dress up top, hip-huggers are all about the peek-a-boo belly. To be sure your huggers are hugging—not suffocating—your midsection, make certain that the waistband sits flat and doesn't create a fold of flesh that hangs over the top.

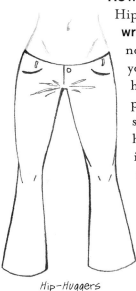
Hip-Huggers

LEATHER PANTS

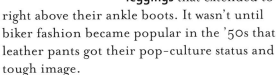
Leather Pants

WHAT THEY LOOK LIKE: Leather pants are generally cut like a second skin to show off the body, with a tight fit in the seat and thighs and tapered legs.

WHO MADE THEM: Some of the earliest leather pants were the genius of Native American women who wrapped their legs in animal skins, creating **leggings** that extended to right above their ankle boots. It wasn't until biker fashion became popular in the '50s that leather pants got their pop-culture status and tough image.

WHO MADE THEM HOT: Channeling renegade rock god Jim Morrison, tough girl Angelina Jolie seemed to practically live in her leathers during her Billy Bob Thorton years. But unlike Morrison, who admitted to rarely changing his pants, Jolie's been seen in many different pairs of leathers.

HOW TO ROCK THEM: If you want to sport leathers without looking too biker chick, follow Anne Hathaway's style of juxtaposing slinky leather with a tweed jacket in the 2006 film *The Devil Wears Prada*. However you wear your leather, it's best to keep it simple.

LOW-RISE JEANS

WHAT THEY LOOK LIKE: These jeans' waistline falls an inch or more below the belly button. There are different names for different styles—like ultra-low rise, for example—which

indicate just how low they go. The shorter the placket (strip of fabric holding the zipper or button fly), the lower the rise.

WHO MADE THEM: Around 1993, British designer Alexander McQueen created what he called bumsters—pants cut so low, they exposed the top of the crack. It took a few years for the look to infiltrate the denim department, but in the late '90s, boutique jean lines like Earnest Sewn and Frankie B. began producing slightly more modest versions of low-rise jeans—a look soon loved by J. Lo, Gwyneth Paltrow, Charlize Theron, and other Hollywood heavyweights.

WHO MADE THEM HOT: Mariah Carey created her own low-rise jeans by cutting off the waistband and wearing them in her 1999 "Heartbreaker" video.

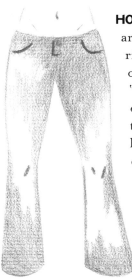

HOW TO ROCK THEM: There are two rules to wearing low-rise jeans: 1) Be conscious of exactly *how* low they're "rising" and 2) be careful of the dreaded muffin top—squeezed flesh that hangs over the sides. If either is a problem, opt for a slightly higher waistline or bigger size. Pair them with a long **A-shirt**.

Low-Rise Jeans

OVERALLS

WHAT THEY LOOK LIKE: Often made of sturdy fabrics like denim, corduroy, or a heavy cotton twill, overalls are loose pants that have an attached bib and shoulder straps that fasten near the clavicle.

WHO MADE THEM: Overalls, the uniform of carpenters, bricklayers, and other laborers, have been commonplace in the US since their inception. But it wasn't until WWI that overalls were marketed to women working in factories. In 1914, Lee made womanalls in khaki fabric and Levi Strauss & Co. followed suit with its own launch of Freedomalls in 1918.

WHO MADE THEM HOT: In the 1990 film *Ghost*, Demi Moore played the ultimate cool artist—she lived in a huge New York City loft, was a master potter, wore overalls often, and, despite being a mourning young widow, looked fabulous doing it.

HOW TO ROCK THEM: Try a wide-strapped **tank** or **crop top** beneath your overalls to girlify them. Wearing them with long-sleeve collared shirts or oversized **T-shirts** can cause a Farmer John effect.

Overalls

Hazardous Pants

Jeans are usually known as comfort clothing, but in 2003 a Canadian doctor wrote to the *Canadian Medical Association Journal* about the dark underbelly of too-tight low-rise pants. He reported that some of his patients experienced a tingling sensation on their thighs and all had been regularly wearing tight low-rise jeans for more than six months. The too-tight jeans had been pinching a sensory nerve under the hip. Once the women wore looser pants, the pain went away.

PALAZZO PANTS

Palazzo Pants

WHAT THEY LOOK LIKE: These wide-legged pants are cut close to the body at the waist and gradually flare out toward the ankle. Hemlines hit anywhere from mid-calf to the ankle.

WHO MADE THEM: Palazzo pants first made waves in the 1930s, when Carole Lombard wore them while golfing with her husband, Clark Gable, at the Riviera Country Club in LA. The style evolved so that all well-to-do women like Lombard would have something to wear while playing sports.

WHO MADE THEM HOT: Ditching the dress altogether, Ingrid Bergman attended the 1975 Oscars wearing a chiffon top, palazzo pants, and a scarf. Her outfit is still regarded as one of the most classic and inventive Oscar ensembles in history.

HOW TO ROCK THEM: Because of the billowy nature of these pants, it's best to wear something form-fitting up top, like a simple shell, to keep from looking like a big ol' sack.

Saint Laurent is the one who gave women the tailored, formal pantsuit in 1966. By the 1970s, pantsuits had flooded mainstream fashion and become the new uniform for working women. Oddly, high-end restaurants wouldn't serve women wearing pants back then, which must have made it tough for ladies to power lunch with the boys.

Pantsuit

WHO MADE THEM HOT: Diane Keaton's role in the 1977 film *Annie Hall* inspired women to pick out pantsuits of their own. Proving suits weren't just for boardrooms, Bianca Jagger famously gave the style a sexy spin by wearing hers sans **blouse** when out clubbing at Studio 54.

HOW TO ROCK THEM: Pantsuits are so versatile in their design that they can work on any body, but the bigger your size, the wider a pant leg you should go for.

PANTSUITS

WHAT THEY LOOK LIKE: This tailored jacket-and-pants combo can have many looks, from the wide-legged polyester **trouser** and wide-lapelled jackets of the '70s to the slim-cut velvet jackets and pants that Tom Ford made popular in 1996 when designing for Gucci.

WHO MADE THEM: Coco Chanel dressed herself in pantsuits in the 1920s and '30s, but Yves

PARACHUTE PANTS

WHAT THEY LOOK LIKE: These pants are typically made with (you guessed it) parachute material—a ripstop nylon that is extremely lightweight yet sturdy. Pick either a generous, baggy cut—think MC Hammer circa 1990—or a tight fit and tapered leg, as pictured on the next page. Above all, parachute pants always sport plenty of zippered pockets for storing cargo and providing a bit (or a lot) of bling.

WHO MADE THEM: Denim company Bugle Boy introduced parachute pants in 1983, selling them for $50 a pair. Seemingly overnight, the pants that looked more spacewalk than catwalk were everywhere and Bugle Boy had increased its annual sales from $10 million to $80 million. By 1985, however, the sales plummeted, and a few years later the company went bankrupt. The original style went out, but less flamboyant versions of zippered pants have reemerged since.

Parachute Pants

WHO MADE THEM HOT: In the mid- to late-'90s, TLC put parachute pants back in the limelight by performing in them at shows like the Grammys, MTV Music Awards, and Nickelodeon Kids Choice Awards.

HOW TO ROCK THEM: The key to rocking parachute pants and not looking like you've just woken up from a generational slumber is to look for styles that contain elements similar to the original without the loud, blatant '80s excess. Outfitters like Abercrombie & Fitch, for example, make parachute-cargo pant hybrids called paratroopers, which include a zipper here or pull cord there, but manage to look thoroughly modern.

The Zipper's Long Road

Living in the golden age of gadgets, a time when it seems like new and improved music players are released monthly, it's hard to believe that a simple gizmo like the zipper took more than 50 years to perfect. But it did.

Elias Howe, the American inventor of the sewing machine, patented the earliest form of the zipper in 1851, calling it an "automatic continuous clothing closure." The zipper saw little progress until Whitcomb L. Judson marketed his Judson C-curity Fastener 40 years later at the 1893 Chicago World's Fair. Judson's version jammed easily and turned out to be a commercial flop.

Finally, in 1913, the modern zipper, with its joining metal teeth, was invented, thanks to Universal Fastener Company, which had hired a designer to retool Judson's version. Soon, zippers were turning up on military uniform **trousers**, raincoats, and swim trunks. B.F. Goodrich Company finally coined the term *zipper* when it put the fasteners in its rubber boots and called them the zipper boot in 1923. The name is a perfect example of onomatopoeia—it came from the zipping sound the fastener makes when it is pulled shut.

PEDAL PUSHERS

Pedal Pushers

WHAT THEY LOOK LIKE: Pedal pushers are straight-cut pants that fall right below the knee.

WHO MADE THEM: After WWII, pedal pushers became a lady's only proper attire for bike riding—hence the name.

WHO MADE THEM HOT: In the height of her fame, Marilyn Monroe spent downtime in pedal pushers and a button-up shirt tied at the waist.

HOW TO ROCK THEM:
To sport an updated version of Marilyn's look, wear these pants with a **white crisp dress shirt** like Uma Thurman's in the 1994 film *Pulp Fiction*.

SAILOR PANTS

WHAT THEY LOOK LIKE: Instead of featuring zippers or other fasteners, these wide-legged pants have buttons laid out in a square panel at the tummy. The oversize buttons form an up-side-down U in the front.

WHO MADE THEM: The US Navy introduced sailor pants as part of its uniform in 1901.

WHO MADE THEM HOT: Gwen Stefani, ever the style renegade, has worn big-buttoned sailor pants to several red carpet events.

Sailor Pants

HOW TO ROCK THEM: Instead of pairing sailor pants with nautical stripes, try an ultrafemme sheer **blouse**.

STIRRUP PANTS

WHAT THEY LOOK LIKE: These skintight and tapered pants have an elastic band at the bottom of each leg that wraps under the foot.

WHO MADE THEM: It's reported that those who fought in the battle of Waterloo in the early 1800s wore stirrups. In terms of more casual dress, the first stirrup-like pants were created by designer Emilio Pucci in 1947. They were actually

Stirrup Pants

ski pants that he designed for his girlfriend. By the '60s, the style became a fad, which eventually went out of style only to be resurrected 20 years later by designers like Ralph Lauren and Max Azria of BCBG.

WHO MADE THEM HOT: During the '60s, Mary Tyler Moore wore stretch stirrup pants on *The Dick Van Dyke Show*. In the '80s, the decade most associated with stirrup pants, pop stars like Debbie Gibson made them a must-have.

HOW TO ROCK THEM: Like **leggings**, stirrup pants can be very tight, very thin, and very unforgiving. If you don't feel comfortable wearing them on their own, pair yours with a **miniskirt**.

STOVEPIPE PANTS
(AKA SKINNY JEANS)

WHAT THEY LOOK LIKE: These tight-fitting cotton pants are fitted from the waist and seat right down to the ankles.

WHO MADE THEM: Stovepipes were a signature of the skinny suit (designed by Dougie Millings) that the Beatles made popular in the '60s.

WHO MADE THEM HOT: Though rockers like the Beatles and the Rolling Stones were the first to put stovepipes on every 1960s hipster's most-wanted list, the skinny, tapered pant has had quite the revival in recent years, thanks to

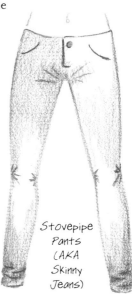

Stovepipe Pants (AKA Skinny Jeans)

Christian Dior designer Hedi Slimane, who has made stovepipes that Sarah Jessica Parker and Nicole Kidman wear. Never one to choose baggy clothes, Posh Spice's pants are the modern-day equivalent to stovepipes: skinny jeans.

HOW TO ROCK THEM: Since stovepipes seem to elongate the leg, you can get the most mileage out of them by pairing them with **stiletto heels**. To dress them down, throw on a pair of **Chelsea boots**.

STRAIGHT-LEGGED JEANS

WHAT THEY LOOK LIKE: No flaring, tapering, or tricky stitching here—these jeans are simply cut straight from top to bottom. The waistline can sit right at the waist or below, depending on the rise.

WHO MADE THEM: Laborers first wore the straight cut (think carpenter pants), but in the 1950s, teens lifted the look for themselves, wearing straight-legged jeans rolled up with **sneakers**.

WHO MADE THEM HOT: Gwyneth Paltrow, Uma Thurman, and other late '90s fashion queens created a hot market for straight-legged designer denim.

Straight-Legged Jeans

HOW TO ROCK THEM: From sneakers to pointy-toed **pumps**, straight-legged jeans offer the widest array of shoe compatibility.

Denim in Distress

Back in the day, denim lovers had to "break in" their own jeans by running them over with a car, or do a little preshrinking by sinking them to the bottom of a lake. Now, the denim companies do all the dirty work for us—and charge a premium for it. Here are some treatments your blues must undergo.

acid wash ❶ for a sharp contrast of dark and white crinkled-looking streaks, they get a pumice stone—soaked in chlorine bleach or potassium permanganate, not acid—scrub.

raw denim ❷ no prewash, treatment, or distress. Since Lee introduced prewashing to the US in 1973, raw denim jeans are hard to find. If you do buy clothes made of raw denim, make sure to buy them big—they'll shrink considerably without a prewash treatment.

sandblasted ❸ for strategically placed holes and rips, they're weakened via sandblasting with aluminum oxide.

stone wash ❹ to soften the fabric and give it a broken-in look, they're washed with enzymes and stones. It's believed that Nudie Cohn, a former costume designer who created authentic cowboy looks for films, first washed denim with pumice stones in the early '70s.

whiskered ❺ to make permanent crease marks in the fabric, they're wadded up, dipped in resin, and baked in an oven for about 10 minutes.

SWEATPANTS

WHAT THEY LOOK LIKE:
These lounge and exercise essentials are made of cotton, terry cloth, or fleece. They typically have an elastic waistband and may or may not have a drawstring. They fit loosely and often have elastic cuffs at the ankles.

WHO MADE THEM:
Sportswear companies looking to cash in on the jogging boom of the 1970s first made sweatpants and sweatshirts, which were precursors to the nylon jogging suit.

Sweatpants

WHO MADE THEM HOT: The jogging-crazed ladies of the '70s, like Jackie O., wore sweat suits while jogging in Central Park.

HOW TO ROCK THEM: Despite the fact that even America's most glamorous first lady wore sweatpants, it's tough to make this workout wear look stylish off the court or outside the gym—no matter what's spelled out in rhinestones across the butt. But when comfort or a chill wins out over style, sweats qualify as a new best friend.

TRACK PANTS

WHAT THEY LOOK LIKE: These flat-front, straight-legged running pants have an elastic waistband for easy dressing and undressing and are often made of nylon, velour, or fleece. Many styles feature side zippers or snaps on the outside of the leg that run from the hem to mid-calf so athletes can remove their pants without taking off their **sneakers.**

WHO MADE THEM: Tracksuits (consisting of pants and a long-sleeved, lightweight jacket) were developed in the 1950s and used by athletes. Adidas then introduced its classic nylon and polyester tracksuit with the company's signature three stripes in 1975. But the trend really took off throughout the '80s and '90s when sportswear companies like Sergio Tacchini outfitted tennis champs Jimmy Connors, Andre Agassi, and Pete Sampras in stylish and breathable nylon track pants and zip-ups to help keep them warm when practicing. This new style became a huge fad in America that was embraced by everyone from amateur baseball players to Brooklyn street kids to hard-core couch potatoes.

WHO MADE THEM HOT: Break-dancers, Run DMC, and other breakout hip-hop artists in the '80s brought the track pants their initial fame. More recently, Madonna has been photographed wearing old-school Adidas track pants off-duty. In the early 2000s, reality stars on *Laguna Beach* and *The Real Housewives of Orange County* lunched around Southern California in Juicy Couture's velour versions.

Track Pants

HOW TO ROCK THEM: They work with **flip-flops** and, of course, **sneakers.** But don't try to turn track pants into something more glamorous than what they are by wearing them with **heels**, **wedges**, or platform sandals.

The First Female Slack-ers

Long before Marlene Dietrich or Katharine Hepburn donned slacks and **trousers**, sharp-shooting outdoorswoman Calamity Jane bucked convention by wearing britches just like the boys. After traveling to the West with her family, and honing impressive shooting skills along the way, Jane joined the US Army (a move that was virtually unheard of for women in the 1860s). Because the army had no uniforms for ladies, she was outfitted in regulation men's trousers. In the following years, as she battled Native Americans alongside Buffalo Bill and Wild Bill Hickock, and helped create the town of Deadwood, South Dakota, she did so in pants—never again returning to her petticoat and skirt-dressing ways.

TROUSERS
(AKA SLACKS)

WHAT THEY LOOK LIKE: In the US these are pants with wide legs, cuffs, front pleats, and pockets, and are typically made of heavy materials like tweeds and wools. In Great Britain, however, the word *trousers* is used in the place of pants and has a much more general definition.

WHO MADE THEM: In 1913, designer Paul Poiret was one of the first to design pants for women, making wide-legged trousers he called harem pants, based on those worn for centuries by women of Far Eastern countries like China and Malaysia. Coco Chanel, one of the first women to wear her boyfriends' trousers, later made similar versions for women to wear while playing sports.

WHO MADE THEM HOT: Legendary French stage actress Sarah Bernhardt, who was known for playing male roles, was one of the first actresses to wear pants in public, way back in the 1870s. In the 1930s, it was still considered scandalous for a woman to wear pants, but Katharine Hepburn, who wore her first pair of trousers at age 8, wasn't afraid to go against the grain. Though film studios wanted to see her decked in glamorous dresses, Hepburn always donned pants offscreen—a move that, in 1986, won her a lifetime achievement award from the Council of Fashion Designers for personal style.

HOW TO ROCK THEM: To emulate the picture-perfect look of Bree (from *Desperate Housewives*), wear trousers with **twinsets**. If you're aiming for a more rough-and-tumble effect, wear slouchy slacks with a vintage Def Leppard **T-shirt** and **slipper flats**.

Trousers
(AKA Slacks)

TUXEDO PANTS

WHAT THEY LOOK LIKE: These black suit pants have a satin stripe that runs down the outside of each pant leg.

WHO MADE THEM: Yves Saint Laurent adopted the pinnacle of men's formal wear for women in 1966.

WHO MADE THEM HOT: The tuxedo pants that Marlene Dietrich wore in the 1930 film *Morocco* represented an unprecedented wardrobe choice for women in the movies. The role, one of her first in American film, cemented her status as a standout star—an achievement no doubt helped by her memorable look in the movie.

HOW TO ROCK THEM: To tame the tuxedo pants' black-tie effect, pair them with a super-soft **T-shirt** and leopard-print flats.

Tuxedo Pants

YOGA PANTS

WHAT THEY LOOK LIKE: To flex, bend, and move with the best of yogis, these pants are typically equipped with a flat (not bunched) elastic waistband that sits on the hips. They are often cut like **boot-cut jeans**—fitted along the legs, then slightly flared at the bottom. They're made of stretchy Lycra-cotton blends to help the shape of the pant retain memory through the most intense yoga practice.

WHO MADE THEM: The yoga pant was the first exercise pant designed with fashion in mind (unlike boring **sweats**, for example). In 1999, the style hit the mainstream, when even J. Crew got into the yoga game, offering yoga pants as a part of its first-ever gym wear collection. In 2000, athletic clothing designer Chip Wilson opened the first Lululemon, a now international chain of boutique stores specializing in high-end yoga clothing, specifically yoga pants. Supermodel-turned-yogi Christy Turlington also helped bring yoga wear to the masses when she launched a yoga clothing line, Nuala, in conjunction with Puma in 2002.

WHO MADE THEM HOT: Famous yogis like B.K.S. Iyengar and Pattabhi Jois may have brought the physical practice of yoga to the US from India, but they weren't wearing yoga pants when they did it. Rather, it was paparazzi shots of rock-hard celebs like Madonna and Jennifer Aniston traveling to and from their workouts that put yoga pants on the fashion map.

HOW TO ROCK THEM: Just because they're called yoga pants doesn't mean you can only do yoga in them. These pants are great for any kind of exercise or for just lounging around the house. Because they are low-waisted, it's best to pair them with a long, fitted **T-shirt** (or **tank**, if you are in a yoga class) to ensure full belly coverage.

Yoga Pants

SHORTS

BERMUDA SHORTS

WHAT THEY LOOK LIKE: These long shorts look like flat-front **trousers** cut just above the knee. Though they were originally made in solid khaki (think of the shorts UPS employees wear), plaids and colorful prints soon became standard Bermuda-making material.

WHO MADE THEM: When the British military was stationed in Bermuda around 1900, the hot climate demanded that they wear shorts—instead of pants—as part of their uniforms. The look caught on and, by 1920, even local businessmen were chopping the legs off their pants to help beat the heat.

WHO MADE THEM HOT: In the '50s, Bermuda shorts were unavoidable—college kids, vacation-ing golfers, and entire families were decked in them. Actress Doris Day was often outfitted in Bermuda shorts, **knee socks**, and proper sweaters, spawning thousands of copycat darlings to sport her goody-two-shoes look.

HOW TO ROCK THEM: Depending on the type of fabric they're made of, Bermudas can be dressed down or dressed up. If you're working with solid Bermudas that look more business than day-at-the-beach (think khaki or pinstriped fabrics), pair them with pointy heels and a wispy **blouse**. If your Bermudas are cotton and color-ful, pair them with **flat-soled sandals** and a **polo shirt** for a more laid-back look.

Bermuda Shorts

BOARD SHORTS

WHAT THEY LOOK LIKE: These polyester-blend swim trunks are usually cut low on the hips. Their hemline can fall anywhere from mid-thigh to right below the knee.

WHO MADE THEM: Swim trunks have been around for guys since the 1930s, but in 1993 surf company Quiksilver launched Roxy, a line for the ladies, and introduced women's board shorts as part of its debut.

WHO MADE THEM HOT: Michelle Rodriguez, Kate Bosworth, and the kick-ass cast of surfers in 2002's *Blue Crush* took on the guys and waves in board shorts and bikini tops.

HOW TO ROCK THEM: Wear your board shorts with a **tank** or bikini top when surfing, playing volleyball, or running surfside. Unlike bikini bottoms, these stay-put bum covers are the perfect type of beachwear for girls who do more than just tan on the sand.

Board Shorts

DAISY DUKES

WHAT THEY LOOK LIKE: These jean shorts are essentially denim **hot pants**. They're cut so high that the inseam is a next-to-nothing inch long.

Daisy Dukes

WHO MADE THEM: Though hot pants had been around for more than a decade, the denim version hit its peak after the character Daisy Duke paraded around in them in the 1979 TV show *The Dukes of Hazzard*. Actress Catherine Bach made many of her own costumes herself, highlighting her best physical attributes and making her a bona fide calendar girl. During the show's run, her poster outsold that of even Farrah Fawcett, the ruling poster queen at the time. Eventually, her little shorts came to be known as "daisy dukes."

WHO MADE THEM HOT: This one's a no-brainer: Catherine Bach as Daisy Duke. Jessica Simpson picked up the tiny-short torch in the 2005 film version of *The Dukes of Hazzard*.

HOW TO ROCK THEM: In real life, it's hard to wear daisy dukes without looking a little trailer trash. Your best bet is to keep your top half respectably covered. As fashion-crazed Victoria "Posh Spice" Beckham has said, "However you're built, be mindful of the rule that if you get your boobs out, put your legs away and vice versa." Amen!

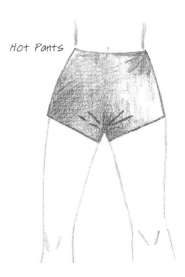

Hot Pants

HOT PANTS

WHAT THEY LOOK LIKE: These second-skin supershort shorts traditionally fit high on the waist near the belly button.

WHO MADE THEM: European ladies of the night (prostitutes, nightclub dancers) first wore short shorts in the '20s and '30s, but it wasn't until 1970 that the style went from risqué to OK-for-day, quickly saturating the local streets. *Women's Wear Daily* dubbed the tiny shorts "hot pants" and, by 1971, American women were donning them too. James Brown even recorded a song that year called "Hot Pants." (The B-52s and the Donnas also put out songs about hot pants.)

WHO MADE THEM HOT: Before the long security lines and the carry-on restrictions, flying the friendly skies was all about glamour. In the 1960s, legendary designer Emilio Pucci created uniforms of knee-high boots and hot pants for Braniff Airways flight attendants, who then became known as Puccis Galore—after the *Goldfinger* siren Pussy Galore. Southwest Airlines also got in on the game, outfitting their sky waitresses in orange hot pants and **go-go boots**—a uniform that eventually found its way into the Hooters

restaurants of today. In 1994, the Vatican officially welcomed the term hot pants into Latin vernacular with the words *Bracae brevissimae* (bracae-trousers and brevissimae translate to "very short").

HOW TO ROCK THEM: Though women of the '70s wore hot pants to work, this look is best suited for off-duty hours. Because they show so much leg, hot pants should be paired with a long-sleeved top. **Tights**—black, white, or brightly colored—can help make hot pants more modest, and **knee-high socks** will help show off knees and thighs.

MADRAS SHORTS

WHAT THEY LOOK LIKE: These shorts are made from a textured cotton plaid called madras. The fabric's basket weave produces a bumpy feel. Classic madras shorts are often cut long like **Bermudas**, though many are made with thigh-high hemlines. A popular madras look is a patchwork style made with squares of different types of plaid.

WHO MADE THEM: Though the fabric comes from Madras, India, sportswear company Brooks Brothers is credited for first bringing the colorful fabric to American wardrobes in 1920.

WHO MADE THEM HOT: College kids on Ivy League campuses in the 1950s rocked madras shorts en masse, helping to make it an American prep wear classic.

HOW TO ROCK THEM: Because the fabric is so lightweight and colorful, madras shorts are suited for summer. Like any busy pattern, madras shouldn't be worn from head to toe; wear a solid shirt in a mellow color (like icy blue or white) to keep from looking like a train wreck of patterns and hues.

Madras Shorts

Pants Patterns to Know

pinstripe ❷ a fabric that's fashioned with super narrow lines. Pinstripes are popular in suits and slacks.

plaid ❷ a fabric woven with yarn-dyed fibers that produce a criss-cross pattern. Types include tartan (used in the Scotch Tape logo), argyle (a diamond design), check (Burberry's signature nova plaid), and harlequin (color-blocked squares).

seersucker ❷ like madras, seersucker (a word whose Persian root translates to "milk and sugar") is a textured fabric often patterned with thin stripes and used for making **clam diggers** and other summery pants. Brooks Brothers introduced it to the US in 1830.

BELTS

Back in the 16th century, men wore "military girdles," what we consider the first belts; they were basically bands worn around the waist to hold weapons and keep clothes in place. In the 1850s, this concept infiltrated women's fashion, and dresses were adorned with sashes made of matching fabric and meant to be worn around the midsection. Then, in the early 1920s, the dropped waists of flapper fashion pushed belts to the back of the closet. They soon returned in the '30s and '40s, however, as more women started wearing pants.

Today, belts come in all kinds of shapes and materials: wide, narrow, leather, ribbon, chain, and canvas. They are a staple in every girl's closet, often helping us keep our pants up or adding that extra bit of flair—and always drawing attention to our waists.

BIKINI CHAIN
(AKA BELLY CHAIN)

This fine gold chain worn with a bikini bathing suit or **hip-hugger pants** was introduced in the late 1960s as a bikini chain. In the mid '90s, it came back on the scene as the belly chain, a hybrid jewelry piece and belt adornment, which was sold in surf shops and national accessories stores like Claire's. Worn for both trips to the beach and formal events, the belly chain was seen on Jada Pinkett Smith at the 1997 Oscars (hers was decked with diamonds) and Shakira, who shook things up with her US release of the "Whenever, Wherever" video in 2001. In 2004, designer Kimora Lee Simmons sported a belly chain in her 2004 Baby Phat ad campaign, and Beyoncé Knowles has been photographed donning one with a bikini while on vacation in France. A belly chain boasts versatility, too—it can also be worn around the neck.

COWBOY BELT
(AKA TOOLED LEATHER BELT)

The handmade, leather cowboy belt is traditionally wide with embossed motifs. Like **cowboy boots**, it has Mexican and Central American origins and was a popular style worn by local *vaqueros*. Of course, it was onscreen cowboys like John Wayne, Clint Eastwood, and TV's the Lone Ranger who brought cowboy belts into style. Bruce Springsteen posed for his 1984 *Born in the USA* album in a studded cowboy belt, and music legend Dolly Parton wears hers with supertight

pants and chest-busting button-up shirts. Stars of the noncountry set like Christy Brinkley and pop singer Jewel know how to put a feminine spin on the manly standard by pairing cowboy belts with dresses.

GAUCHO BELT

This chunky belt flashes literal bling—it's made of metal medallions or coins joined with leather and chain. Gaucho belts, which originated in South America during the 19th century, are named for the Argentinean horsemen, or gauchos, who wore them on the plains. Since being imported to the States in the '70s, the gaucho belt has remained an exotically flashy addition to dresses and jeans. In the early 2000s, Christian Dior got into the gaucho act, creating medallion-adorned belts and bags that were worn by Kate Moss.

MILITARY BELT
(AKA WEBBED BELT)

Made of heavy canvas webbing fastened with a clip buckle, the military belt has been used by the armed forces for decades, but it was adapted for casual wear by men and women in 1960. Since the early '80s, the look has become popular with propagators of Latin street style, who wear military belts with Dickies and white **A-shirts**. (Reese Witherspoon nailed the look in the 1996 movie *Freeway*.) Clothing companies have picked up on the trend, manufacturing these belts with their logos emblazoned on the buckle.

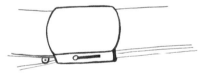

Military Belt
(AKA Webbed Belt)

LINK BELT

The link belt can be made of either chain links or round, oversize medallion-type links, as shown here. Both can be worn with the excess chain or remaining links hanging down to one side. This look has been a popular part of Southwestern style, propagated by Ralph Lauren's collections, since the '80s. Starlets like Selma Blair have belted them over simple white dresses to bring attention straight to the waist.

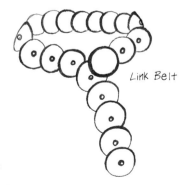

Link Belt

OBI BELT

This wide, wraparound cloth belt has been part of the Japanese kimono ensemble for centuries. Western fashionistas adopted the belt in the '80s and wore it with long shirts to help create a waist for both casual and formal occasions. To add drama to an outfit, wrap the obi around your waist, cross it in back, and knot its braided cords or wide sash end pieces in the back or front. Use it to add shape to a straight-cut dress like Natalie Portman and pop singer Rhianna have done on the red carpet, or to add a little flair to a **wrap shirt** worn with slim-cut **trousers**.

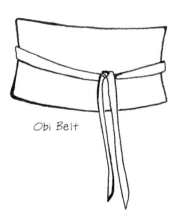

Obi Belt

SASH

These long, wide strips of soft fabric are wrapped around the waist or hips to tie in a knot or bow. Researchers at the University of Illinois have reported that more than 25,000 years ago women of the Ice Age wove and wore sashes. In modern times, sash belts play a role in formal and informal dressing. In 1932, sash belts were introduced to prep school uniforms, and, six years later famed fashion designer Claire McCardell put sash belts on her flowing bias-cut dresses. This belt has made a comeback in the 2000s with stars like Kylie Minogue, Sienna Miller, Mandy Moore, and Naomi Watts using them to wrap around minidresses and '50s-style frocks.

RIBBON BELT

This belt's band is made of grosgrain ribbon and is cinched by pulling the end through double D-shaped rings. Traditionally, this type of belt has been popular with the golfing set, but in the early 2000s, clothiers Abercrombie & Fitch and J. Crew resurrected the look. Though the belt is made with a simple strip of ribbon and a few metal rings, it can sell for upwards of $20. For those who are DIY-inclined, there are instructions online that tell you how to make your own—all you really need are a couple of pieces of grosgrain ribbon, D rings, and thread.

Ribbon Belt

SKINNY BELT

In the 1950s, the skinny belt—a belt just a half-inch or quarter-inch thick—was the pièce de résistance for the ladylike outfit. TV favorites Lucy and Ethel wore skinny belts at the waists of their **shirtdresses**. Fashion icon Audrey Hepburn added skinny belts to her tea-length dresses in the '50s. After being supplanted by casual dressing, grunge chic, and super-**low-rise pants** for decades, the cinched-waist look came back in the 2000s. Trendsetters like Helena Christensen, Angelina Jolie, Charlize Theron, and Kirsten Dunst have all used skinny belts to accentuate their teeny-tiny middles.

Skinny Belt

STUDDED BELT

This leather belt adorned with silver studs has its roots in punk rock. The Ramones, the Sex Pistols, and a slew of other CGBG-bound rockers made this hard-edged look popular among '70s rebels who would rather die than disco. Modern-day pop stars like Kelly Clarkson and Avril Lavigne who try to sell themselves as hotshots-with-an-edge do it with studded belts, Converse All Stars, and radio-friendly pop songs. Studded belts can also toughen up an otherwise frilly outfit. In a fresh fashion move, Shakira wore a studded belt over a skintight halter dress at the MTV Europe Music Awards in 2005, combining a glam nightlife look with a classic street style.

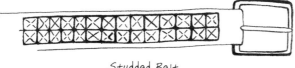

Studded Belt

SHOES
A Girl's Best Friend

Marilyn Monroe is known all too well for cooing, "Diamonds are a girl's best friend." But it seems that she (or whoever wrote the score for *Gentlemen Prefer Blondes*) forgot about shoes. If you look in any modern girl's bedroom, chances are you'll find a whole lot more in the way of shoes than you will in the way of shiny, expensive, expertly cut precious stones. In fact, the average American woman owns 30 pairs of shoes. How many girls do you know who own 30 diamonds (or *any* gem for that matter)?

Shoes have gone from being functional and protective footwear to the total attention-getter of the outfit—and sometimes the most expensive piece. When Carrie Bradshaw, fashion icon and *Sex and the City*'s lead character, was mugged, the assailant demanded not only her handbag and jewelry, but also her **strappy sandals**.

Women's obsession with shoes is not merely a recent one, either. It began as far back as the mid-16th century when Henry II's wife, Catherine de' Medici, started sporting high heels (traditionally worn only by men) and, consequently, turned them into a fad for women. Catherine loved how they

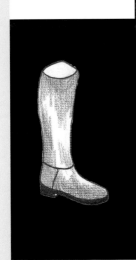

made her look thinner and taller —and she was definitely on to something: The structure of a high-heeled shoe gives a woman an instant posture makeover. Our chests stand taller, our legs appear longer, and our butts get a lift—pretty drastic results for just a simple change in footwear.

We also adore our shoes because, unlike our pants size, our shoe size doesn't change —no matter how many pints of ice cream we eat. And despite the pinched toes that *stilettos* bring or the blisters caused by a new pair of *wedges*, that's a comforting thing.

Finally, there's something alluring about the foot itself. The study of reflexology suggests that each section of a foot corresponds with different parts of the body. If the heel represents the pelvic area and the bottoms of our big toes the brain, we are pampering our entire being by throwing on a comfy pair of Birkenstocks. And even if you don't buy into reflexology, consider this: The foot has 26 bones and thousands of nerve endings, making it one of the most sensitive parts of our bodies. With all those nerve endings susceptible to touch, the feet hold our body's most underrated pleasure points. Naturally, we love to treat our feet—it's little wonder that, in the process, we've become seduced by the shoes themselves.

CHAPTER GLOSSARY

broguing ❷ small holes punched in the leather for decoration, often across the toe.

insole ❷ inside of the shoe that supports the bottom of the foot.

top lift ❷ the bottom of the heel that meets the ground.

vamp ❷ the front part of the shoe.

SHOES

BALLERINA FLATS

WHAT THEY LOOK LIKE:
Usually covered in satin
or made from patent
leather, ballerina flats
are round-toed slippers
with a thin sliver of a sole.

*Ballerina
Flat*

WHO MADE THEM: In 1944,
designer Claire McCardell commissioned
Capezio to make ballet slippers with a design
that could be worn on the street. Since they are
made with a minimal amount of materials, and
virtually no leather, they were also a smart choice
for 1940s designers who were facing financial
restrictions during wartime.

WHO MADE THEM HOT: Audrey Hepburn—
once a ballet dancer herself—wore these flats in
iconic movies like *Sabrina* and *Funny Face*.

HOW TO ROCK THEM: Ballet flats look great
with just about anything, from a thin **wrap
shirt** and **miniskirt** to a **turtleneck** and tailored
trousers or skinny jeans. For a really classic look,
take a cue from Ms. Audrey and wear them with
capri pants and a boatneck cotton top.

CHELSEA BOOTS

WHAT THEY LOOK LIKE: These ankle boots can
have either square or pointy toes, and elastic
sides for easy foot insertion and removal.

WHO MADE THEM: Though Chelsea boots were
first produced in the 1950s, it was London's
custom shoemaker Anello and Davide who
created the Beatles' famous boots. The company
still makes custom shoes for anyone who stops by
its St. Christopher Place shop.

WHO MADE THEM HOT: In 1964, the clean-cut
Beatles wore these boots on an American tour,
bringing them to the mainstream. Later, the Fab
Four sported their own riff on the Chelsea—a
similarly styled boot with a higher heel and side
zipper. That boot became so popular, it was
known as the Beatle boot.

HOW TO ROCK THEM:
Wear them—or any ankle
boots—with skinny pants
and a black sweater for
a clean, mod look.

Chelsea Boot

Words Inspired By Shoes

bootlegger ❷ before it became synonymous with
illegal downloaders, the term *bootleggers* was used
to signify 17th- and 18th-century lawbreakers
smuggling contraband across borders inside
their boots.

cop ❷ police officers became known as cops
because of the copper-tipped boots they wore.

gumshoe ❷ in the early 1900s, *gumshoe* became
slang for detective, since detectives wore boots
with gum-rubber soles.

CLOGS

WHAT THEY LOOK LIKE: The word *clog* comes from an old word (origin unknown) that meant "clump of wood"—and if you own clogs, you know how well the name fits. The clog has a chunky wooden sole that is curved to support the arch of the foot, a round toe, and no back—just slide it on. The vamp is usually made of leather.

Clog

WHO MADE THEM: The earliest wooden clogs are said to date back to 6000 BC, though it's not clear who wore them. In the 17th century, clogs were commonly worn as shoe coverings, to protect delicate slippers from mud and dirt.

WHO MADE THEM HOT: From the 1800s to the 1940s, clog dancing (which eventually evolved into tap dancing) was all the rage in England —even Charlie Chaplin was a clogger at the time. By the 1960s, the psychedelically dressed hippies who attended Woodstock and other free-love gatherings had brought clogs into everyday casual wear, and they have remained there ever since. Clogs have also become the shoe of choice for chefs who need comfort plus serious traction to avoid taking a dive on the slippery restaurant kitchen floor—which often gets littered with spilled liquids and wayward food as the night wears on.

HOW TO ROCK THEM: Take a cue from the original hippies and don them with a long wrap skirt or jeans.

COMBAT BOOTS

WHAT THEY LOOK LIKE: Lots of height. Thick leather. Rugged rubber soles. These boots just scream power—they *were* designed for soldiers, after all.

WHO MADE THEM: Though combat boots were first developed for the soldiers of WWII, it's Dr. Martens that has become fashion's—and music's—most beloved rugged bootmaker. Since the 1960s, ska freaks, grunge rockers, punk mavens, and even straight-edged devotees have co-opted the company's classic eight-eye boot with rubber "bouncing" soles as wardrobe must-haves for their respective style tribes.

WHO MADE THEM HOT: Garage rock princesses of the '90s like Bratmobile, L7, and members of Hole portrayed their kick-ass image by wearing combat boots. Thora Birch and Scarlett Johansson were dressed as fashionable misfits in the 2001 film *Ghost World*.

Combat Boot

HOW TO ROCK THEM: You can wear combat boots with almost anything, from jeans to plaid skirts. Pair these clunky numbers with long girlie floral dresses or **baby dolls** and other above-the-knee hemlines to toughen up a little-girl look.

COWBOY BOOTS

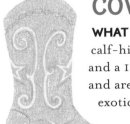

Cowboy Boot

WHAT THEY LOOK LIKE: These calf-high boots feature pointy toes and a 1½- to 2½-inch angled heel and are made of rugged leather or exotic skins like crocodile or lizard. These boots were designed with heels to prevent the shoes from sliding forward through a saddle's stirrups and with loose openings above the calf so they could be kicked off easily. A shorter, bootie version (the demi-boot) became popular for a spell in the 1990s—women could get the rugged look of jeans-over-cowboy boots without the bulk above the ankle.

WHO MADE THEM: The cowboy boot is a well-traveled shoe. It first came to Mexico via Spanish conquerors, then from Mexico to the US. In the mid-1800s, Kansan and Texan boot-makers created custom leather boots for ranch hands who were herding cattle along the trail that stretched, well, from Texas to Kansas.

WHO MADE THEM HOT: Though men proudly wore high heels in the 16th, 17th, and 18th centuries, this is the only modern-day high-heel shoe for men that passes as rugged, tough, and socially acceptable. It's no surprise that the original style mavens of cowboy boots were the hard-as-nails Western film legends Roy Rogers, John Wayne, Clint Eastwood, and Robert Redford. Later, John Travolta wore them in *Urban Cowboy* (1980). A kick-butt Uma Thurman famously escaped being buried alive by kicking off her slick cowboy boots, which were tied together, and then pounded herself out of a makeshift casket in the 2004 film *Kill Bill Vol 2*. Hollywood pop princesses Britney Spears and Jessica Simpson stick to their country roots by regularly sporting cowboy boots.

HOW TO ROCK THEM: Tried-and-true cowboy boot pairings include the ultra-American **boot-cut jeans** and **T-shirt** combo or the Southern-belle-gone-bad look of boots and a denim **miniskirt**. For a more romantic look, try the Ralph Lauren approach, pairing your boots with a **prairie dress**.

DRIVING SHOES

Driving Shoe

WHAT THEY LOOK LIKE: Shoes worn by race car drivers inspired this design. Similar to **moccasins**, the driving shoe is a type of **loafer** that features flexible leather soles. Both the heel and sole are dotted with rubber studs to help prevent slippage when putting the pedal to the metal.

WHO MADE THEM: Though some historians say the first driving shoe may have been created as early as the 1960s by Carshoe, a Prada-owned company, Italian shoemaker J. P. Tod is most often credited with establishing this style. After its 1979 launch, the shoe went from a must-have for European race car drivers to a highbrow fashion statement for both men and women, regardless of the number of rpms clocked.

WHO MADE THEM HOT: While pricey driving shoes have been a footwear favorite for the well-to-do, it's the daredevil race car drivers who have given this funny-looking loafer an edge. Today, Danica Patrick and other Indy 500 racers zoom around the track in driving shoes.

HOW TO ROCK THEM: Create a relaxed but highbrow look by wearing a **polo shirt** and **boyfriend jeans** with driving shoes.

ESPADRILLES

WHAT THEY LOOK LIKE:
A cross between a sandal
and a **wedge**, the
espadrille is the
quintessential
summer shoe.
The upper is made
of a soft fabric and is stitched to a wedge sole
and features wide laces that wrap and tie around
the ankle.

Espadrille

WHO MADE THEM: In 1970, Andre Assous and
Jacques Cohen brought this traditional Spanish-
style shoe from Europe to the US market after
noticing that the only fabric shoes American
women were wearing in hot weather were foot-
confining and sweat-producing tennis shoes.

WHO MADE THEM HOT: Jet-setters and beach-
combers of the 1970s put espadrilles on the
map—the style was more sophisticated than the
flip-flop, but just as summer friendly.

HOW TO ROCK THEM: Espadrilles are breezy
and beautiful with cotton dresses, shorts, and
other hot-climate wear.

Combating Evil With a Teeny Slipper

A centuries-old European superstition dictated
that new homeowners were to place a child's
shoe in the wall near a door or window to
guard against evil spirits that may be roaming
their new property. Sound looney? The trend
was strong enough to make its way to the US.
The proof: Tiny shoes have often been found
inside the walls of New England houses during
major renovations.

FLAT-SOLED SANDALS

WHAT THEY LOOK LIKE: These are open-toed,
strappy shoes with flat soles.

WHO MADE THEM: The flat-soled sandal is one
of the oldest shoes in the book, dating back to
around 7000 B C. One just has to look at Jesus'
and Moses' feet in biblical art to get a sense of
how incredibly long this style has been around.

WHO MADE THEM HOT: German shoe
company Birkenstock—known as the ultimate
in ergonomic, ecological, and breathable
footwear—brought its shoe to the US in the
mid-'60s, promoting its Arizona sandal—a
backless, open-toed sandal that featured two
buckled straps that reach across the top of the
foot. Though the clunky, unglamorous shoe was
declared horrific by followers of high fashion,
hippies, orthopedic doctors, and stay-at-home
moms went crazy for the organic cork and rubber insoles that were made to mold to your feet.
Birks came back into style in the early '90s when
nouveau hippies paid upwards of $100 per pair.

HOW TO ROCK THEM: Sandals are definitely a
warm weather shoe to be worn barefoot; despite
what many Europeans
do, keep your sandaled
feet sock-free. Wear
them with **caftans**
and **tunic dresses** for
a super-relaxed look.

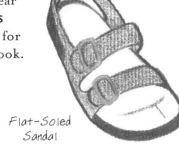
Flat-Soled
Sandal

FLIP-FLOPS
(AKA THONGS)

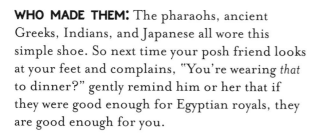

Flip-Flop (AKA Thong)

WHAT THEY LOOK LIKE: This is the simplest of sandals—just a flat sole with a thong construction between the toes.

WHO MADE THEM: The pharaohs, ancient Greeks, Indians, and Japanese all wore this simple shoe. So next time your posh friend looks at your feet and complains, "You're wearing *that* to dinner?" gently remind him or her that if they were good enough for Egyptian royals, they are good enough for you.

WHO MADE THEM HOT: The beach boys and girls of the '60s surfer culture catapulted flip-flops into popularity.

HOW TO ROCK THEM: Flip-flops may take some getting used to for those who are new to them, but they are the lazy dresser's dream—no straps! no fasteners!—and go with just about everything. A nice pair of metallic leather thongs can even work for a night on the town.

Soldiers of Style

According to ancient Greek historian Polybius, it's not just the ladies who have a history of shoe obsession. He wrote that Greek and Roman soldiers were so concerned with the condition and appearance of their sandals that commanding officers had to remind them to pay attention to the condition of other things—like their weapons—when heading into battle.

GLADIATOR SANDALS

WHAT THEY LOOK LIKE: This flat-soled, open-toed sandal crawls up the leg to typically the ankle or below the knee. It features straps that extend across the foot and buckle around the ankle or leg. A variation includes extra-long leather laces that are wrapped and tied along the calves.

WHO MADE THEM: This type of sandal was first worn by the Roman army in 35 AD. While the regular members of the army wore low-strapped sandals, the officers wore sandals with above-the-ankle straps. Roman emperor Gaius Caesar wore his sandals studded with gold and silver. He was so known for his favorite style of shoe, known then as "the calige," soldiers began to call him Caligula. Gladiator sandals were popular in Greece at the same time.

WHO MADE THEM HOT: Tara Subkoff, actress and designer for clothing label Imitation of Christ, brought gladiator sandals back to the masses when she designed a pair for Easy Spirit in 2004.

HOW TO ROCK THEM: Gladiator sandals that crawl toward the thigh look great with short shorts and a long-sleeved top. For a more casual look, pair your gladiators with a summery **sundress** and a pair of shades.

Gladiator Sandal

GO-GO BOOTS

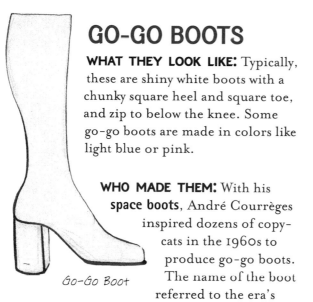
Go-Go Boot

WHAT THEY LOOK LIKE: Typically, these are shiny white boots with a chunky square heel and square toe, and zip to below the knee. Some go-go boots are made in colors like light blue or pink.

WHO MADE THEM: With his **space boots**, André Courrèges inspired dozens of copycats in the 1960s to produce go-go boots. The name of the boot referred to the era's energetic disco dancing. America's first discotheque, the Whiskey A Go-Go, which opened in Hollywood in 1963, dazzled clubgoers by employing **miniskirted**, go-go boot-wearing dancers to perform in cages suspended above the action. Anyone hoping to emulate the go-go dancers, *had* to purchase their shiny boots.

WHO MADE THEM HOT: Nancy Sinatra wore white patent go-go boots on television when singing her 1966 hit *These Boots Were Made for Walkin'*. After that, club kids and wannabes helped make the go-go boot the best-selling shoe of the decade.

HOW TO ROCK THEM: At your next theme party, emulate the typical '60s go-go girl by wearing your boots with a minidress and mod makeup.

GRANNY BOOTS

WHAT THEY LOOK LIKE: These lace-up or button-up ankle boots feature a low heel and narrow toe. The name lends itself to the style worn by bespecled grandmas, like those found in *Little Red Riding Hood*.

Why Social Climbers Preferred Heels

Back in the 16th century, the first heels stood only about an inch tall, but over the next two centuries, they crept up to three inches. Because only the elite could afford to have heels made for them, the rich began to be known as "well heeled." Of course, the rich enjoyed being the only ones who could afford to wear high heels because it meant that the poor had to literally look up to them. Snooty alert!

WHO MADE THEM: A follow-up to the walking boot, made popular at the end of the 19th century, the buttoned granny boot was the hottest fashion for elite and working-class women alike at the dawn of the 20th century. In the '60s, this style regained popularity with a laced version (as pictured below).

WHO MADE THEM HOT: Fleetwood Mac singer Stevie Nicks brought a dark edge to Victorian-revival dress with her granny boots, handkerchief-hemmed skirts, and all-black attire.

HOW TO ROCK THEM: Granny boots are a favorite of alterna-girls and goth goddesses. Steal their look by wearing your grannys with long, flowing skirts in dark, brooding colors.

Granny Boot

JELLIES

WHAT THEY LOOK LIKE: Named for their jellyfish-like translucence and their jellylike feel, these usually colorful rubber shoes come in either slipper or typical sandal form.

WHO MADE THEM: Jellies were born in Brazil and first introduced to the US at the 1982 Knoxville World's Fair. They were an instant hit with chicks who couldn't get enough neon or synthetic materials into their wardrobes.

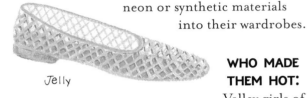

Jelly

WHO MADE THEM HOT: Valley girls of the '80s paired loudly colored jellies with side ponytails and plastic jewelry.

HOW TO ROCK THEM: Jellies are a perfect nod to summer and work great in non-active situations—like sitting poolside with some pals. But unless they're lined with absorbent fabric, keep them in the closet on blisteringly hot days since your feet are bound to slide in the shoe when conditions get especially sweaty, causing shaky soles and foot stink. What's more, rubber straps can be notoriously flimsy and break easily: a pretty embarrassing way to twist an ankle.

LOAFERS

WHAT THEY LOOK LIKE: This casual slip-on shoe is fashioned much like a **moccasin**, with classic U-shaped stitching that covers the top of the foot, but unlike moccasins it has a heel and a sturdy wooden sole.

Loafer

WHO MADE THEM: In 1936, American shoemaker George Henry Bass made one of the first loafers and produced the gold standard of the style with the Weejun (short for Norwegian—the shoe's birthplace). Soon after, the company began to sell loafers with pennies placed in the front slots. The penny loafer was a must-have for preppy students in the 1950s—you know, back when you could actually buy something, like a piece of bubble gum, for a penny.

WHO MADE THEM HOT: James Dean is well known for having sported the penny loafer and **motorcycle jacket** combo around town in the 1950s, and Michael Jackson (famously pairing them with white socks) helped revive the loafer during his 1980s "Off the Wall" and "Thriller" years. In the '80s, Gucci produced loafers for the moneyed set. They immediately became the decade's most popular status symbol for men wanting to flash their wealth.

HOW TO ROCK THEM: The loafer is the quintessential preppy shoe. Wear it with pearls and/or **pleated skirts** for style points and smarts.

Louis Heel

LOUIS HEELS

WHAT THEY LOOK LIKE: A Louis-heeled shoe can be a **mule**, **Mary Jane**, or boot. Its distinguishing feature is its 1½-inch curved heel that widens at the top.

WHO MADE THEM: King Louis XIV of France, who ruled from 1643 to 1715 and measured about 5' 6" tall, had his favorite designer, Jean Bérain, make him special wooden heels covered in red leather, which only he and his

court were permitted to wear. By the mid-18th century, when King Louis XV reigned, a take on the block heel became popular for women, this time curved inward with a fatter footprint. The style became known as the "Louis" heel.

WHO MADE THEM HOT: This type of heel was most popular in the '20s, as fair-legged flappers wore curved heels with straight-hanging dresses.

HOW TO ROCK THEM: Because the heel has a blocky look, these shoes work well with longer hemlines and heavier fabrics, like wools and tweeds.

Mary Jane

MARY JANES

WHAT THEY LOOK LIKE: With their rounded toes, slipper construction, and bar strap across the top of the foot, Mary Janes are the original schoolgirl shoe and the all-time favorite of curly-haired cuties like Annie and Shirley Temple.

WHO MADE THEM: Mary Janes were named after Mary Jane, a character in the Buster Brown comic strip, who wore this type of shoe. In 1904, owners of the massive Brown Shoe Company bought the rights to the Buster Brown comics (coincidentally they were both named "Brown") after meeting the comic book creator Richard F. Outcault at the Saint Louis World's Fair and used the comic to market the Mary Jane shoe.

WHO MADE THEM HOT: Mary Janes were strictly produced for children until the 1960s youthquake (see page 11) darlings picked up on the kiddie trend and started donning little girl-inspired dresses to go with their little girl-inspired shoes. In the '90s, Courtney Love rocked her "kinderwhore" look that involved pairing Mary Janes with **baby-doll dresses** and ripped **tights**. Mary Janes have since evolved to include styles with high and/or chunky heels.

Mary Jane High Heel

HOW TO ROCK THEM: Baby-doll dresses still look cute with Mary Janes, but for a more modern look, try pairing them with knee-length A-line skirts, **tights**, and an ironic **T-shirt**.

How Mary Jane Got Her Shine

Ultrashiny patent leather is one of the most popular materials used to make Mary Janes. To create the shiny finish, layers of dyes, oils, varnishes, and/or resins are applied through a process developed in 1818. By the end of the century, patent leather became a popular material for the footwear of wealthy schoolchildren and adults. By the 1950s, the material was widely used for the footwear of children of all economic classes.

MOCCASINS AND MOCCASIN BOOTS

WHAT THEY LOOK LIKE: Authentic mocs are soft-soled **loafers**, but other twists include up-to-the-knee and ankle-boot styles. While many modern-day versions have rubber soles, traditional features like beading, leather fringe, and a molded fit remain common.

WHO MADE THEM: These leather slippers were first stitched, beaded, and worn by Native Americans at least 10,000 years ago. In 1978, Australian shoe company Ugg created its own take on moccasin boots, making a version from sheepskin with hard soles and shearing lining.

WHO MADE THEM HOT: With their soft soles and supercomfy fit, moccasins are the next best thing to going barefoot. No wonder this etho-chic style became an immediate hit with boho hippies of the 1960s.

HOW TO ROCK THEM: Be like British "it" girls Kate Moss and Sienna Miller, and slip on boot-style moccasins over skinny jeans and a tunic top.

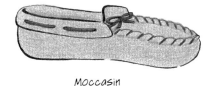

Moccasin

MOTORCYCLE BOOTS (AKA HARNESS BOOTS)

WHAT THEY LOOK LIKE: These rugged black boots traditionally feature a square toe and a leather harness that is joined by an O-ring on the outside ankle of the boot.

WHO MADE THEM: Century-old boot company Frye's created the first motorcycle boot in 1938 for a US navy admiral. The admiral's new shoe, then called a harness boot, caught on within the forces and Frye's began to fill orders for other soldiers serving in WWII, including General George Patton. This sturdy black boot eventually became popular within the '50s biker culture and has remained a motorcycle rider's shoe of choice ever since.

WHO MADE THEM HOT: Motorcycle boots became a hot commodity after Marlon Brando was seen wearing them in his 1953 film *The Wild One*. Later, in 1955, pop band the Cheers released the song "Black Denim Trousers and Motorcycle Boots," a cautionary tale of a rebel teen dying in a motorcycle accident after he "took off like the devil" on California's Highway 101, the same road where James Dean died in a car accident (also in 1955). And, of course, Catwoman pounced around in this ready-for-action footwear, along with her leather cat suit and goggles, in original DC Comics.

HOW TO ROCK THEM: To wear motorcycle boots with jeans is a no-brainer. You can also switch up the look by wearing them with a wispy chiffon **slip dress** and a mess of delicate necklaces.

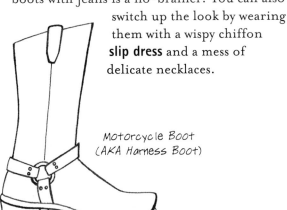

Motorcycle Boot
(AKA Harness Boot)

MULES

WHAT THEY LOOK LIKE: A mule is a hybrid of a **clog** and a heel. Though it's backless and closed-toed like a clog, the mule is a bit more refined in the sole department, tending to have **pump** or **stiletto**-type heels rather than a carved wood sole. The vamp fits snugly across the top of the foot.

Mule

WHO MADE THEM: Men wore mules in the 16th century, but women didn't until the 17th century. For a woman to expose a naked foot was considered scandalous, so mules were deemed quite sexy. They were extravagant shoes made of silks and satins, and featured rich embroidery. An 1865 painting by Édouard Manet titled *Olympia* showed a prostitute wearing nothing but a stylish pair of mules; the painting offended conservative Parisians who felt the image cheapened the traditional style of painting nudes.

WHO MADE THEM HOT: A favorite of the *Sex and the City* wardrobe department, mules soared in popularity after the fictional Carrie Bradshaw repeatedly rocked Manolo Blahnik mules on the show.

HOW TO ROCK THEM: Mules look great with pants and dresses of all lengths, but there's one crucial rule to remember: These slide-ons are best with bare feet—exposing a **stocking**-clad heel is a major fashion don't.

OXFORDS

WHAT THEY LOOK LIKE: This square or round-toed lace-up shoe is a predecessor of the saddle shoe. The low-heeled style has just a few lace holes and sometimes features broguing across the toe. Oxfords are shaped like saddle shoes, but they don't feature the saddle's signature two-toned, **spectator**-style coloring. A variation of the traditional oxford is the wing tip, which has a contrasting color of leather on the toe that's shaped like the top of a heart. First designed in the early 1900s, the wing tip often has lines of tiny punched-out holes along the toe.

WHO MADE THEM: European men wore the first oxfords in the 1640s. However, the style didn't get the actual oxford name until a couple of centuries later, when men at Oxford University began sporting them. In both the United States and Europe, the oxford quickly earned respect for being the most stylish and practical men's walking shoe. By the end of the 19th century, women were wearing them to play sports. And by the 1920s, the female version was decked with thick, square heels and often used for dancing. The oxford is well-known as the ultimate gender-bender shoe for its manly characteristics (such as broguing).

WHO MADE THEM HOT: Amelia Earhart wore oxfords, as did Marlene Dietrich, who was famous for sporting menswear from her top hat right down to her oxfords.

HOW TO ROCK THEM: For a rockabilly-inspired look, pair oxfords with thick **bobby socks**, a flirty dress, and ultra-glam makeup.

Oxford

PLATFORMS

WHAT THEY LOOK LIKE: Platforms have an exaggerated stacked sole and thick heel that give the style a funky edge. The raised overall height of the sole decreases the angle of the foot (in a four-inch-heeled shoe, the heel may be raised two inches higher than the ball of the foot instead of four), making it easier to wear than other towering shoes.

WHO MADE THEM: Admit it: When you think of platform shoes, full-blown '70s disco madness comes to mind. But actors in ancient Greece first wore platforms because it allowed them to be better seen on stage by theatergoers in the back rows. They were also worn by Venetian and Turkish women in the 16th century (their shoes, called chopines, stood as tall as two feet!) Stateside, Salvatore Ferragamo created the first platform craze in the late '30s. He used layered cork soles (like those of the **wedge** from the '20s) due to the European leather rationing of WWI.

WHO MADE THEM HOT: In the '70s, glam rockers Elton John and David Bowie famously performed in platforms that towered six inches high. Disco queens like Diana Ross were fanatics for sparkling platforms, and in 1972 designer Harold Smerling introduced his aquarium-like platforms—a style that was proudly worn by Flyguy in the 1988 movie *I'm Gonna Git You Sucka*. Jodie Foster famously wore her platforms with **hot pants** when playing a teenage prostitute in the 1976 film *Taxi Driver*. In 1993, fashion designer Vivienne Westwood created a silk ribbon lace-up mock-crock shoe, with a sole that was nearly 10 inches high, for supermodel Naomi Campbell to wear when sashaying down the catwalk in Westwood's fall Anglomania show. The impossibly high shoe proved to be tough strutting for even a pro like Naomi—she took a good fall that night. (And you thought it was painful to wear three-inch heels!)

Platform

HOW TO ROCK THEM: Because they elongate the leg, platforms show off your assets best when paired with short shorts and **miniskirts**. They also look great with flared pants, like **bell-bottoms**.

PUMPS

WHAT THEY LOOK LIKE: A type of **slipper shoe**, often with a pointy toe and a midsize to low heel.

WHO MADE THEM: These days, the term *court shoes* connotes athletic shoes worn on tennis or basketball courts, but back in the 12th century, court shoes, or shoes women wore while visiting royalty, were simply pointy shoes with two-inch heels—the precursor to today's pumps. The style reemerged in the early days of Hollywood with the help of shoemakers like Salvatore Ferragamo and David Evins (aka the King of Pumps), who often dressed Tinseltown's earliest superstars, like Mary Pickford, in this style of shoe.

WHO MADE THEM HOT: Who didn't! Grace Kelly wore pumps when marrying the prince of Monaco, first ladies Nancy Reagan and Jackie Kennedy wore them to inaugural ceremonies, and the working women of the '80s strutted a **stiletto** version (with a U-shaped foot opening and pointy toe) in offices nationwide.

HOW TO ROCK THEM: Because they vary so much in heel height and material, different pumps work with different things. Try pointy-toed pumps with micro-minis and round- or square-toed pumps with sophisticated **pantsuits**.

Pump

Pump Variations

Unlike **wedges** or **espadrilles**, pumps are made in a dizzying array of types with different distinguishing factors. Here are a few popular variations:

kitten heel ❶ a very low heel, less than an inch tall.

peep-toe ❷ a shoe with a cutout at the tip to allow a toe or two to peek out. One of the most popular styles in the '30s.

sling back ❸ a backless pump with a strap that wraps around the heel.

T-bar shoes ❹ a slipper-style shoe that features two straps—one runs across the arch of the foot and another runs down the foot from the arch to the toe or tip of the shoe. This type of shoe was first popular in the '20s and '30s.

RIDING BOOTS

WHAT THEY LOOK LIKE: These round-toed boots reach the knee and feature a low, thin heel. Designers often make a street-style variation of riding boots with flat soles.

WHO MADE THEM: Riding boots have been around since the 16th century when warlords wore them while on horseback. Throughout the centuries, the British royal set pushed the equestrian look, pairing riding boots with **jodhpurs** and **blazers** for everything from hunting to show jumping.

Riding Boot

WHO MADE THEM HOT: When Elizabeth Taylor wore riding boots in the 1944 movie *National Velvet*, girls everywhere wanted to emulate her character, Velvet Brown—riding boots and all.

HOW TO ROCK THEM: These flat-to-the-ground boots look great with an **oxford shirt** and tucked-in jeans.

The Tie That Binds

For centuries up until 1949, Chinese girls would have their toes broken and bound at the age of 3 so that their feet wouldn't grow longer than 10 centimeters. The idea was that if a woman's feet were that small, it would be so difficult to walk that she would be restricted to the house. During the time that this practice thrived, the average woman's shoe in China was only 3 inches long —about the height of an iPod. Women would have to constantly shift their weight from side to side just to keep their balance.

SLIDES

WHAT THEY LOOK LIKE: This backless, high-heeled shoe is similar to the **mule**, but it features an open toe, with just a band of material across the top of the foot to hold the shoe in place (think Barbie). A super-seductive version of the slide called a marabou heel features pastel colors and decorative stork feathers.

WHO MADE THEM: Back in the late 1920s and '30s, Hollywood's leading ladies donned these high-heeled, open-toed shoes as seductive bedroom slippers. They were first called mules because they had the same backless construction, but eventually they became known as slides. In 1970, Candies revived the style, introducing its best-selling slide, which Olivia Newton-John famously wore in the 1978 classic *Grease*.

WHO MADE THEM HOT: In the '30s, slides were the epitome of sexy footwear, in part because movie star Jean Harlow was shown onscreen dangling one provocatively from her big toe. The shoes became so associated with Harlow that they were then known as Harlow slippers. Marilyn Monroe also wore slides in the 1955 movie *The Seven Year Itch*.

HOW TO ROCK THEM: The *Grease* formula is still relevant today —slink into a rocker **T-shirt**, skinny jeans, and barely there slides for a tough but feminine look.

Slide

Did You Know?

American shoemakers only began making shoes specific for left and right feet in 1820. To learn more shoe history, check out Toronto's Bata Shoe Museum's online exhibits at *www.batashoemuseum.ca*.

Hollywood's Twinkle Toes

In *The Wizard of Oz*, Dorothy's iconic red slippers were originally scripted to be silver —but the director wasn't shooting in pricey Technicolor for nothing. He insisted that the shoes' hue be changed from a blah silver to a bright red. It's rumored that up to eight pairs of ruby slippers were made for the film, including an early version with curled toes, à la Aladdin, and a version specifically worn for dancing scenes. A 2000 auction fetched $666,000 for one of the original eight pairs.

Slipper Shoe

SLIPPER SHOES

WHAT THEY LOOK LIKE: This simple flat is a slip-on shoe that hugs the entire foot.

WHO MADE THEM: It's hard to say who first developed the slipper, as it's one of the oldest shoe styles. Popular in the 19th century, slippers have been a bridal wear and fairy-tale staple for centuries.

WHO MADE THEM HOT: In *The Wizard of Oz*, Dorothy Gale's ruby slippers mesmerized a generation of moviegoers. Her shoes were painstakingly made from silk faille covered with georgette fabric and topped with a dazzling 2,300 sequins. Female cartoon characters, like Daisy Duck, Minnie Mouse, and Smurfette, are also known for their slipper-wearing tendencies.

HOW TO ROCK THEM: They're not just for lounging or your wedding day. Slippers look great with **cigarette pants** and the short hemlines of **tent**, **trapeze**, and **smock dresses**.

SNEAKERS
(AKA KICKS OR TRAINERS)

WHAT THEY LOOK LIKE: Whether high-tops or low-tops, canvas, nylon, rubber, or infused with air-suspension systems, sneakers—named for their noiseless soles that allow wearers to sneak by—represent the most American style of footwear.

Converse All Star

WHO MADE THEM: The history of sneakers goes back to the 11th century, when indigenous tribes in South America spread the sap from the rubber tree directly onto the bottom of their feet to waterproof them. The same rubber treatment was used hundreds of years later in the 1860s to make the first sneakers, which had canvas uppers with flexible, waterproof rubber soles. At six times the price of other shoes, the first sneakers were affordable only for the country club elite. Though they became cheaper, that initial price point set the stage for decades of high-priced, status-setting designer kicks.

WHO MADE THEM HOT: America's original sneaker mogul and basketball player Chuck Taylor helped create the world's first athletic shoe in 1917—which soon became the official shoe of the NBA. Though retired from the courts, the Converse All Star—nicknamed Chuck Taylors or Chucks—is *still* a streetwear staple and one of the brand's best-selling shoes. Canvas sneakers became an off-court phenomenon in the 1950s, when street-savvy teens paired them with rolled-up jeans. In the '80s, Michael Jordan followed in Chuck Taylor's footsteps when he worked with Nike to create the world's most sought-after basketball shoe, Air Jordans.

Reebok Freestyle Sneaker

HOW TO ROCK THEM: The king of casual footwear works best with jeans or **trousers**, but if you are gutsy, feel free to wear them with just about anything.

Sneaker Timeline

1916 ❷ The United States Rubber Company introduces the Keds sneaker.

1917 ❷ The Converse All Star becomes the first shoe designed for the sport of basketball.

1938 ❷ Keds releases its classic Triumph shoe.

Keds Triumph Shoe

1970 ❷ Companies like New Balance go beyond simple canvas and rubber construction and introduce materials like breathable nylon.

1971 ❷ The Nike swoosh logo is created by graphic design student Carolyn Davidson (who was paid a mere $35 for her services).

1982 ❷ Reebok launches the freestyle sneaker — *the* aerobic shoe of the '80s.

1985 ❷ The Air Jordan I hits shelves. Since only white shoes are allowed on NBA courts, the black high-top with the red swoosh is banned from professional play. Jordan wears them anyway and has to pay a fine each time he breaks the rules.

1989 ❷ Reebok introduces the Pump sneaker, injecting air-pump technology and a custom fit into the performance-shoe category. The pricey $179 kicks have the most successful product launch in the company's history and sell 20 million pairs in the first four years.

2006 ❷ Nike teams up with Apple to create the Nike+, a microchip-equipped shoe that gives runners biofeedback info via their iPod nanos.

2007 ❷ The San Francisco Bay Area rap group the Pack releases "Vans" on its *Skateboards to Scrapers* EP.

Sock Stars

Like socks? Here are a few of the more inventive styles that keep us on our feet.

ankle ❷ the favorite of runners, these stop at the ankle.

bobby ❷ popular in the '40s and '50s, these thin ankle socks have a turn-down cuff.

knee-highs ❷ first worn with knickers by boys in the 1900s, these below-the-knee socks became popular with **miniskirt**-wearing teens and women of the '60s.

over-the-knee ❷ an elastic top holds up these extra-long pull-up socks that reach over the knee.

Peds (aka socklettes) ❷ Peds is the trademarked name for thin, low-cut nylon socks that can't be seen when worn with **pumps**. Other styles of Peds are designed specifically for wearing with **mules** (they cover the toe area and ball of the foot only) or with slides (they cover the top arch and ball of the foot).

Over-the-Knee

Ped (AKA Socklette)

scrunch ❷ think leg warmer with a foot attached — the sock to rock in the '80s.

trouser/dress ❷ thin, lightweight, originally designed for men, and made of silky fabrics.

Trouser / Dress

SPACE BOOTS

WHAT THEY LOOK LIKE: Though they are called space boots, these shoes look nothing like the big clodhoppers worn by NASA's frequent-fliers. This lightweight boot is white, flat-soled, and reaches only as high as the calf.

WHO MADE THEM: Designer André Courrèges created the space boot in the 1960s; it's considered the original **go-go boot**. Space boots are shorter than go-go boots (which cover the calf), feature a small, rectangular cutout on top, and have a lower heel. Designers haven't put too much energy into reviving the space boot since its debut, so the style sighting is rare these days. But they're still considered one of the most inventive boot designs of the 20th century.

WHO MADE THEM HOT: Mod hipsters of the '60s paired them with **miniskirts**, pale lips, and brightly painted lashes for the first wave of future chic.

HOW TO ROCK THEM: Display vintage know-all by donning space boots with an A-line **shift dress**.

Space Boot

SPECTATORS

WHAT THEY LOOK LIKE: Take the two-toned palatte of a saddle shoe, marry it with a **pump**, and you've basically got a spectator. The toe section of this low-heeled pump is generally painted a darker color than the rest of the shoe. The most popular color combos? Basic black and white or brown and white.

WHO MADE THEM: Coco Chanel created this classy and popular option for the style hounds of the 1920s and '30s.

WHO MADE THEM HOT: Katharine Hepburn was notorious for wearing spectators with her **trousers** in the '30s.

Spectator

HOW TO ROCK THEM: Spectators are best paired with prim and proper outfit pieces, like trousers and **twinsets**.

SPORT SHOES AND SANDALS

WHAT THEY LOOK LIKE: These are characterized by hypertraction-equipped soles, strong Velcro or D-ring and lace closure, and breathable, quick-drying fabrics to withstand wet conditions.

WHO MADE THEM: Mark Thatcher, founder of outdoor sport shoe brand Teva (Hebrew for "nature"), developed a prototype for a river shoe that combined the stability and support of **sneakers** with the quick-drying and open construction of a sandal in 1984. This first sport sandal opened the floodgate for many other styles, including hiking and trail shoes that were lightweight like the sport sandal design, but incorporated a boot's support and coverage. Today, brands like Merrell and Ecco have expanded the sport shoe market.

Sport Sandal

WHO MADE THEM HOT: When you think of sport shoes and sandals, "hot" doesn't exactly come to mind. And it shouldn't. The point of these all-terrain shoes is to get you across the stream and up the mountain, which they do beautifully.

HOW TO ROCK THEM: Wear hiking boots and sport sandals with your sturdiest hiking or river clothes, or with casual **chinos** and **henleys** while on the street.

Stiletto

STILETTOS

WHAT THEY LOOK LIKE: These are **pumps** with slender, spiked heels that are usually three to five inches high.

WHO MADE THEM: In the late 1940s, new technology for making steel rods (called metal extrusion) gave way to an engineering marvel—pencil-thin heels that could miraculously support a woman's weight. A steel rod was injected into the core of the heel, allowing Italian cobblers in the mid-'50s to develop a shoe with a much higher lift—climbing up to five inches. Designer Roger Vivier is credited with inventing the stiletto in the early '50s.

WHO MADE THEM HOT: Silver screen sirens of the 1950s Jayne Mansfield and Marilyn Monroe became queens of the stiletto. In 1971, stiletto master Manolo Blahnik designed his first shoe. By the '90s, his shoes were so popular, they were worn by nearly every celebrity walking the red carpet.

HOW TO ROCK THEM: Modern-day divas like Mariah Carey and Victoria Beckham are notorious for wearing stilettos, jeans, and a **camisole** just about anywhere—from movie premieres to shopping trips in Beverly Hills.

STILETTO BOOTS

WHAT THEY LOOK LIKE: These skintight boots have a **stiletto** heel and are generally made of soft leather that hugs the foot, ankle, and calf.

WHO MADE THEM: Heeled boots have been around since the late 1800s, but their killer-heeled stiletto counterpart first came on to the scene in the 1950s, along with stiletto **pumps**.

WHO MADE THEM HOT: One of the most well-known stiletto wearers was fetish icon and pinup Bettie Page, who wore the edgy boots in photo shoots during the '50s. Over the years, power players have become well-known for donning stiletto boots. Naomi Campbell wore black patent stiletto boots when showing up for community service duty in Manhattan in 2007, and Condoleezza Rice wore a black pair while on the job at Germany's Weisbaden Army Airfield in 2005.

HOW TO ROCK THEM: High stilettos can be made demure by pairing them with a long skirt. If you feel like playing the vixen, wear them with tucked-in skinny jeans and a racy **tank**.

Stiletto Boot

Killer Heels

James Bond isn't the only one with a shoe that doubles as a weapon. Check out the 1992 film *Single White Female* for a scene in which the **stiletto** is used as a fatal weapon.

STRAPPY SANDALS

WHAT THEY LOOK LIKE: These are traditional **flat-soled sandals** with a touch of upgraded glamour, thanks to delicate heels (usually a **stiletto**) and dainty straps across the top of the foot.

Strappy Sandal

WHO MADE THEM: When shoe wizard Salvatore Ferragamo developed metal arch support in the '20s, a closed-toe structure was no longer needed to keep the foot from sliding out. Soon, painted toes were peeking out of the strappy-heeled sandals of A-list actresses like Greta Garbo.

WHO MADE THEM HOT: The ladies of *Sex and the City* made strappy sandals synonymous with city chic, as they donned this style of barely there foot coverings in nearly every episode.

HOW TO ROCK THEM: The delicate nature of these shoes works best with light clothes—think ladylike dresses, not power suits. Wear yours with a classic **wrap dress** and **bangle bracelets**.

WEDGES

WHAT THEY LOOK LIKE: Like the **platform** shoe, the wedge has a stacked wooden, rope, cork, or rubber sole. But while the platform boasts a heel carved out from the sole, the wedge's sole is solid and stacked higher toward the heel to create an arched foot. The upper can be made of anything from clear plastic to supple leather.

Wedge

WHO MADE THEM: Historians trace the wedge's beginnings back to the 16th century, but the towering, modern-day version originated with Salvatore Ferragamo, who conceived the ortho-pedic wedge (with a curved insole to support the arch of the foot) in the mid-'30s. Shoe designer David Evins' multicolored pave (gem-studded) wedges worn in the 1934 film *Cleopatra* also rep-resented a notable first appearance of the style.

WHO MADE THEM HOT: The leading ladies of *That '70s Show* brought the decade's famed foot-wear back in the late '90s, wearing wedges with wrap skirts and loud prints.

HOW TO ROCK THEM: Like platforms, wedges are a great shoe for showing off the leg. Wear them with short shorts, **miniskirts**, and tiny dresses.

WELLINGTONS

WHAT THEY LOOK LIKE: These traditional English rubber boots, also known as Wellies, are easy to pull on, rise right below the knee, and feature a chunky rubber sole.

Wellington

WHO MADE THEM: Arthur Wellesley, a British war hero and the First Duke of Wellington, had a shoemaker create the first Wellingtons in 1817. They were made of leather and cut close to the leg and ankle so they could be worn under narrow pants, unlike other boots at the time. The rubber version we think of today was first worn by soldiers in the trenches of WWI and WWII.

WHO MADE THEM HOT: After a grand shoot-out in her home, a gun-wielding Angelina Jolie wore nothing but her husband's white button-up shirt and Wellingtons when fleeing would-be assassins in the 2005 film *Mr. And Mrs. Smith*. Attendees of the annual and muddy Glastonbury festival in Britain—including Kate Moss—suit up in mud-friendly Wellies and short shorts, bringing sensible chic to the summer event.

HOW TO ROCK THEM: These sophisticated rain boots are a great option in mucky winter weather. Wear them with tucked-in jeans like Lindsay Lohan in the 2006 film *Just My Luck* or on a clear day with safari shorts and a wrap sweater like Spice Girl Geri Halliwell has been seen doing.

Famous Shoe Fiends

***Sex and the City* heroine Carrie Bradshaw** After realizing how extensive her shoe habit is, she quips, "I've spent $40,000 on shoes and I have no place to live? I will literally be the old woman who lived in her shoes."

Imelda Marcos, former first lady of the Philippines A political uprising in 1986 found her fleeing her palace, leaving behind a rumored 3,000 pairs of shoes. She later was quoted as saying, "I did not have 3,000 pairs of shoes. I had 1,060." Suha Arafat, the ex-Palestinian leader's wife, is said to have a shoe collection that rivals that of Marcos.

Noel Gallagher of the band Oasis He has admitted to having more than 100 pairs of Adidas **sneakers**.

Marie Antoinette, queen of France, 1774–1793 Before her gruesome beheading, she was a poster girl for excess, allegedly owning 500 pairs of shoes.

HANDBAGS

In 1790, a new line of **empire dresses** made without pockets popped up on the streets of Paris. These dresses left wearers without a place to put their powder and coins. Thus, the birth of the handbag.

A century later, the leather handbag arrived, just as people were taking to railways for intercontinental travel. The handbag quickly became a symbol of independence because once armed with it, women no longer had to ask a man to hold her things.

As women have become more active and mobile, handbags have become an increasingly popular necessity for bottle-packing moms, file-carrying businesswomen, and everyday girls on the go. Now, as we tote iPods, PDAs, cell phones, gym clothes, makeup, and more, the handbag has become the "it" accessory of the 21st century.

BAGUETTE

In 1997, fashion house Fendi launched the baguette, named for its small, oblong shape and abbreviated strap that enabled one to carry it under the arm like a piece of French bread. The original Fendi version, made popular by the *Sex and the City* ladies, was made in more than 600 versions and in every type of material, from denim to velvet to leather. The bag inspired hundreds of knockoffs, like the one shown here.

Baguette

BIRKIN BAG

A bag similar to the **Kelly** (see next page), the Birkin came into existence in 1984 when actress Jane Birkin, known for her role in the 1966 fashion film *Blow-Up*, broke a basket containing all her gear while on an airplane. Hermès chairman Jean-Louis Dumas was also on the plane, and the mess caused by her broken basket gave him the idea to make a new, modified Kelly with a double strap, more room, and spill-proof sides. It quickly became Jane's signature carryall and has remained a favorite of fashion-loving celebrities like Demi Moore, Victoria Beckham, and Kate Moss. The authentic Hermès versions are pricey, but more accessible and affordable versions have since been made in a beach-friendly jelly plastic material.

CLUTCH

The clutch is the mother of all evening bags. Its slim silhouette embodies sophisticated refinement and demands light packing since it can't carry much more than a lipstick, credit card, and cell phone. Jackie Kennedy regularly carried an envelope clutch to galas when she was first lady. Framed clutches (pictured here) are those firmer, more rigid clutch bags; they have a snap-top clasp and a metal frame to help give the otherwise soft bag its structure.

Framed Clutch

Though the modern-day clutch became popular around 1926 (when it was often beaded in art deco designs), the clutch has its roots in the 18th century when people carried their documents in leather and silk envelopes.

HOBO BAG

The hobo is a soft, slouchy, and oversize bag with a top that droops in the center to form a half-moon shape. It has wide straps and hangs alongside the torso when worn on the shoulder. Hobos

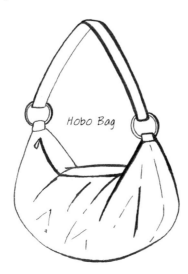

Hobo Bag

became hot in the 1960s when Jackie Kennedy was frequently seen carrying a Gucci version (this Gucci bag eventually became known as the "Jackie bag"). Twenty years later, Liz Taylor, Peter Sellers, and Samuel Beckett showed themselves to be right on point with the hobo trend—they all wore unisex hobos. Gucci resurrected the Jackie bag in 2006 but used the former first lady's maiden name and called it the Bouvier bag.

KELLY BAG

Originally created to hold a saddle, this structured, boxy leather bag features a lock closure and a strap so short it can only be carried by hand. The Kelly bag was once named Haut a Courroies (meaning "bag with tall handles") after Grace Kelly appeared on the cover of *Life* magazine in 1956 and used the bag to block her pregnant belly. Legendary stars like Ingrid Bergman and Marlene Dietrich also carried the Kelly, helping to solidify the style's "it bag" status for generations to come. But the Kelly is not easy to get—the hand-stitched bag takes more than 18 hours to create and costs thousands of dollars. And making it is not the most animal-friendly process, either. To make their alligator skin versions, Hermès uses only leather from the belly and jowls, so it takes *two* whole gators to make *one* Kelly.

MARKET BAG
(AKA THE SHOPPER)

This boxy, oversize tote generally features two straps and is often filled with groceries, TP, and other everyday purchases. With the spotlight on global warming, hybrid cars, and all-around eco chic, 2007 style mavens went wild for the Anya Hindmarch canvas shopper bag that said "I'm not a plastic bag" on its front. Demand for the bag was so high that when it instantly sold out, people began paying more than $400 on eBay for the $15 shopper. The same year, actresses such as Reese Witherspoon, Keira Knightley, and Alicia Silverstone were all spotted carrying shoppers.

Market Bag (AKA The Shopper)

MESSENGER BAG

Messenger bags, a modern take on the newspaper carrier bags of the '50s and similarly styled military surplus bags, first became popular in the '90s with rugged urban bike messengers, who slung oversize bags from brands like Timbuk2 diagonally across their bodies while delivering documents to offices. This renegade look inspired others to ditch their office carry-alls and school backpacks. Soon, posh brands like Kate Spade were producing messenger bags to keep up with the trend. Stylish Hollywood moms such as Kate Winslet have also been known to stock this style of bag full of snacks, bottles, and other kid things for outings with the family. In 2007, Cameron Diaz caught flack for unknowingly carrying a messenger bag with a communist slogan in Peru—a country scarred by former communist occupation.

Messenger Bag

POUCHETTE

Like the **clutch** and some **baguettes**, this small rectangular-shaped bag has just enough room for a phone, a compact, and cash. Its thin, removable strap is so short, the bag falls right under the armpit when worn on the shoulder. While the style first took off with the clutch in the 1920s, brands like Louis Vuitton, LeSportsac, and Coach brought the pouchette craze back with logo-emblazoned styles that were wildly popular in 2000, such as when Jennifer Aniston carried hers to the Academy Awards.

SATCHEL

This structured bag has a hard, flat bottom and a metal frame closure. Its sides angle in toward the top, giving the bag a trapezoidal shape. Doctors once carried this type of bag to make house calls, as did train-riding travelers in the 1850s. But satchels—and the similarly structured carpetbags, made from carpet fabric—became more prevalent after WWI, when opportunity-seeking Northerners who traveled to the South were called carpetbaggers after the style of luggage they carried with them. The fashion died for a while, but by the late 1960s satchels and carpetbags became popular again. Modern-day fashion followers carry satchel styles like Louis Vuitton's Speedy bag, which Jessica Simpson famously took camping in her *Newlyweds* reality show.

Satchel

SHOULDER BAG

This type of handbag, which sits at the hip, has a long strap or chain that is worn over the shoulder. While it comes in many shapes and sizes, the quintessential shoulder bag is Chanel's 2.55, named after the month and year it was introduced. It features a rectangular shape, is made of quilted leather, and has a single chain that can be converted to shorter, double straps. Shoulder bags became wildly popular in the '80s and the 2.55 was no exception. In 2005, the bag was re-released and it quickly garnered a celebrity following—at that time, actresses like Kirsten Dunst were rarely photographed without their chain-strapped shoulder bags.

TOTE BAG
(AKA CARRYALL)

Totes are usually square-shaped bags with an open top and two handles or shoulder straps. L.L. Bean was one of the first companies to design a tote in the 1940s. It was a canvas, two-handled bag they called a boat bag. Later, Enid Collins' signature '60s vintage totes were kitschy, canvas bags with themes such as "Money Tree" (featuring birds under a giant jeweled tree) and "Sea Garden" (featuring sea horses, fish, and kelp). The tote resurfaced again as a must-have when Kate Spade launched her boxy, simple black tote in 1993. More than a decade later, Mischa Barton's character in *The O.C.* used a Chanel tote as a schoolbag, causing high schoolers everywhere to ditch their backpacks in favor of totes.

WRISTLET

The wristlet, with its walletlike slim rectangular body, is equipped with a looped strap that dangles from one end. It can be carried on the wrist, like a purse, or clipped on to a bigger strap of a tote, serving as an easy-to-find wallet. Coach introduced the world's first wristlet in 2001, and people went crazy for its streamlined look and versatile use. The concept was an immediate hit, and first-year sales surpassed expectations. By 2004, Coach was selling 1 million wristlets per year—and inspired countless knockoffs by everyone from Gucci to Target.

UNDERTHINGS
The Foundation of Fashion

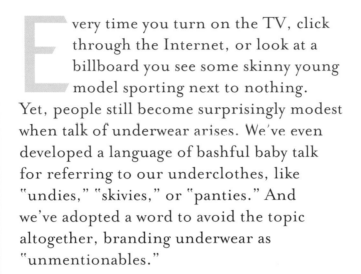

Every time you turn on the TV, click through the Internet, or look at a billboard you see some skinny young model sporting next to nothing. Yet, people still become surprisingly modest when talk of underwear arises. We've even developed a language of bashful baby talk for referring to our underclothes, like "undies," "skivies," or "panties." And we've adopted a word to avoid the topic altogether, branding underwear as "unmentionables."

But if you consider the impact that intimates have on our outward appearance, there's nothing silly or unmentionable about them. From the *corset* to the *slip* to the *padded bra*, underwear is really foundation to make our bodies appear curvier, smoother, or perkier. Let's be real, Jane Russell wasn't born with the cone-shaped breasts she made famous in the 1943 film *The Outlaw*— a spiral-seamed *push-up bra* made that look possible. And the smooth, tight bodies under Hollywood's most form-fitting red-carpet gowns? They're most often molded by suck-it-in *shapewear*.

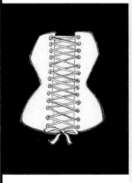

So it makes sense to think of underwear not as a secret subject, but as the building blocks of a great outfit. After all, a too-tight bra can create bulges of back fat on an otherwise even silhouette, and the wrong briefs can leave visible panty lines (aka VPL). It's high time we take our underthings seriously. The next time you get dressed, consider the shape you're building and pick your underclothes as carefully as you do your accessories.

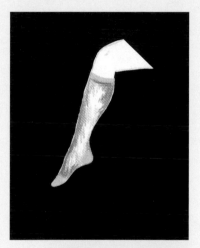

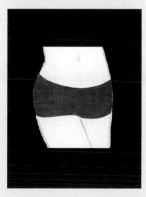

CHAPTER GLOSSARY

bias cut ❶ a diagonal cut across the grain of the fabric. Slips are often cut on the bias. This cut is particularly flattering because it allows the fabric to hang smoothly rather than bunch or ride up on the body.

bodice ❷ the section of a garment between the shoulders and the waistline.

boning ❸ plastic or metal strips placed inside a garment to shape the body and give support.

dart ❹ a V-shaped taper that is sewn into the garment to make it fit closer to the body.

tapered ❺ becomes narrower at one end.

underwire ❻ a flat strip of U-shaped metal or plastic inserted into fabric underneath bra cups to give support.

VPL ❼ a common term for visible panty lines.

whalebone ❽ the bone of real whales was once inserted into **corsets** to support and shape the body.

UNDERTHINGS

BABY-DOLL NIGHTIE

WHAT IT LOOKS LIKE: This ultra-short puff-sleeved nightgown, or nightie, is typically made of sheer fabrics in cream-puff colors. Since it barely covers the bum, the baby doll is often paired with ruffled **briefs**.

WHO MADE IT: Anna Hill Johnstone, costume designer for the 1956 film *Baby Doll*, caused a religious uproar when she put her star in a little girl nightie. New York Cardinal Francis Spellman preached for people to boycott the film after seeing the scene with nightie-clad star Carroll Baker in a crib sucking her thumb.

WHO MADE IT HOT: Despite the cardinal's efforts, Baker started a national craze with her abbreviated nightie, which then took on the name of the film. Later baby-doll darlings include Bridget Bardot and the slumber-partying ladies of *Grease*.

HOW TO ROCK IT: Baby dolls are roomy and loose, so they make great PJs in hot climates. If your baby doll is especially short and has classic lingerie detailing—like ribbons, bows, and superslinky fabric—wear it with **boy briefs** while lounging around the house. You could also borrow the style from Anna Sui's 1990s designs and pair it with **leggings** as a dress—as long as the fabric doesn't look too ready-for-bed.

Baby-Doll Nightie

BANDEAU

WHAT IT LOOKS LIKE: The bandeau is a strapless strip of fabric that covers and flattens the chest to take emphasis off the breasts.

WHO MADE IT: The first bandeaus were fashioned by women themselves, who simply used ribbons or strips of flannel to help flatten the breasts and achieve the highly desired thin and boyish look that was so popular in the late 1910s and 1920s. As the trend caught on, designers started to produce chest-flattening bandeaus, called flatteners, from a combination of cotton and elastic.

WHO MADE IT HOT: In the height of the 1920's androgynous craze, trendy flappers helped popularize the bandeau. Bandeaus are still used by androgony-pushing girls and by gay and transgender women who try to pass in society as men, like Hilary Swank in the 1999 film *Boys Don't Cry* and Felicity Huffman in the 2005 film *Transamerica*.

Bandeau

HOW TO ROCK IT: Bandeaus are a smart choice when wearing a sheer top, **apron dress**, or a **tank** with low-cut armholes.

BIKINI BRIEFS

WHAT THEY LOOK LIKE: These briefs are just like the swimsuit bottom they're named for —high cut on the leg with panels that are connected with inch-wide straps.

Bikini Briefs

WHO MADE THEM: Lingerie companies introduced bikini briefs in the late '60s, after the bikini swimsuit made its debut. The garment's popularity soared in the '70s, when women were wearing skintight pants and doing all they could to eliminate VPL.

WHO MADE THEM HOT: For decades, bikini briefs have remained the most popular style of ladies undies. When re-creating the climactic *Flashdance* audition scene for her smokin' hot "I'm Glad" video, J. Lo danced up a storm in a pair of black bikini briefs and leg warmers.

HOW TO ROCK THEM: The best bikini briefs are made without seams to better help conceal VPL. If your bikini briefs are equipped with thick ribbing or seams, wear them with clothes made of heavier materials that won't expose your underwear's outline—like denim, wool, or fleece.

BOXER SHORTS

WHAT THEY LOOK LIKE: These roomy cotton shorts with an elastic waistband are fashioned after the uniforms of professional boxers.

WHO MADE THEM: Soldiers were given boxers as part of their government-issued uniform during WWI. The soldiers found them so comfy, they kept donning them long after

their service ended. In 1983, *Women's Wear Daily* declared boxers the hot item for women. The same year, underwear trendsetter Calvin Klein created boxers just for women that retained the same shape and feel but offered more feminine lines.

WHO MADE THEM HOT: In the 1985 film *Desperately Seeking Susan*, Madonna wore her boyfriend's boxer shorts, helping make the menswear item a more popular one for the ladies. The members of TLC rocked boxers under their baggy pants circa 1992.

HOW TO ROCK THEM: Boxers are a great option for kicking it around the house. If you have a pair of favorite jeans that are ripped to death, like the kind Nirvana's lead singer Kurt Cobain used to wear, boxers will help cover bits of exposed thigh, crotch, or bum without softening your look.

Boxer Shorts

Captain Commando

Marlon Brando may have created an underwear buzz by scandalously sporting only an undershirt in the 1951 film *A Streetcar Named Desire*, but it was Clark Gable who scared the underwear industry silly. In his 1934 film *It Happened One Night*, he shocked audiences by removing his shirt to show not an undershirt, but his bare chest. It was reported that undershirt sales fell 75 percent after the release of the movie.

BOY BRIEFS
(AKA BOY SHORTS)

WHAT THEY LOOK LIKE: These are shrunken **hot pants** made from stretchy microfiber. They extend about a half-inch past the bum. Up top, they ride on the hips, leaving your belly free to breathe and helping you avoid the stomach-covering effect of the granny panty.

WHO MADE THEM: Lingerie powerhouse Victoria's Secret put boy shorts on display in the mid-'90s. By 2003, the boy short was one of the most popular styles of lingerie. It was in such demand that news headlines questioned whether it would take the place of the **thong** for the VPL-free undie of choice.

WHO MADE THEM HOT: Serena Williams has been known to ditch tennis skirts altogether and wear boy shorts when kicking ass on the court.

HOW TO ROCK THEM: Boy shorts are **low-rise jeans** friendly. Like thongs, they don't leave the dreaded VPL or bunch, nor do they ride up like **briefs**. They stay put like a thong (minus the unpleasant chafing that can occur) and work well with any fitted pants or skirts.

Boy Briefs
(AKA Boy Shorts)

The Commando Experiment

We've all seen the mortifying pictures of young starlets flashing their business without underwear. Not pretty. But consider this: Way, way back in the day (like in the 1700s) going commando was the norm. And for some, it can be a liberating feeling to dare to go bare from time to time. While pulling a Britney or Lindsay is the last thing any self-respecting girl wants to do, there are foolproof ways to skip undies for a day and have no one else be the wiser.

Take a clue from the anti-undie '30s star Jean Harlow and make sure you're covered—that means no **miniskirts**, sheer dresses, or short, full skirts that might blow up in the wind. It might seem like pants would be a good option for the underwear-free, but some fabrics can chafe or give you wedgies. Instead, try a pair of **trousers** or an opaque below-the-knee **pencil skirt** in a dark color to ensure you keep your freewheeling secret safe from unsuspecting eyes.

BRIEFS
(AKA GRANNY PANTIES)

WHAT THEY LOOK LIKE: Briefs have a waistline that hits near the belly button or higher. The legs fall an inch or so below the hips.

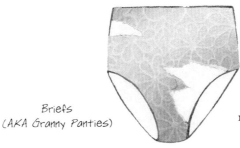

Briefs
(AKA Granny Panties)

WHO MADE THEM: No one designer made briefs. Knee-length knickers simply became shorter and shorter through the 1920s until they had reached the length of panties in the '30s, resulting in the birth of briefs.

WHO MADE THEM HOT: Marilyn Monroe standing on a metal grate, her dress blown up to reveal her brief-style knickers, is an image that's still considered hot today. In 2001, a curvy Renée Zellweger gave old-fashioned briefs a bit of a comeback as the stylistically challenged, yet sexy Bridget Jones.

HOW TO ROCK THEM: These are the tighty whities of women's underwear. They provide full bum coverage and often come in supercomfortable cotton—the perfect companion to **sweats**, pjs, and other loungewear. However, they also fit high on the waist, which is a deal breaker for **low-rise** lovers.

BUSTIER

WHAT IT LOOKS LIKE: This strapless waist-shaper fits tight from the bust to the waist. Many bustiers are implanted with boning to keep their structure stiff. If you've got cleavage, this will push it to the limit.

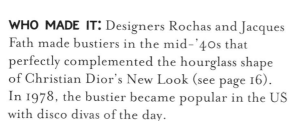

Bustier

WHO MADE IT: Designers Rochas and Jacques Fath made bustiers in the mid-'40s that perfectly complemented the hourglass shape of Christian Dior's New Look (see page 16). In 1978, the bustier became popular in the US with disco divas of the day.

WHO MADE IT HOT: Wonder Woman fought crime in a bustier, Claudia Schiffer modeled a black lace bustier in, according to Mike Myers and Dana Carvey in *Wayne's World*, a "shwing-worthy" Guess ad, and Britney Spears famously wore a bustier with shoulder straps at the MTV Music Awards when she kissed Madonna onstage.

HOW TO ROCK IT: A bustier can look great with anything from **low-rise jeans** to short shorts. No matter how you wear it, keep in mind the message the bustier sends: "Hey everyone, check out my rack!" It can be a fun look at a party, but not exactly the vibe you want to give off at a job interview.

CAMISOLE

WHAT IT LOOKS LIKE: This **tank top** made of cotton or silky material often has adjustable, bralike straps and classic lingerie touches like lace trim or rosettes.

WHO MADE IT: The camisole simply evolved from the **corset** cover—a similar-looking garment, usually with a pleated front, that was layered over the corset and under the clothes to help provide warmth.

WHO MADE IT HOT: The camisole's celluloid moment: Nicole Kidman's no-frills Egyptian cotton version, made by lingerie company Hanro of Switzerland, in Stanley Kubrick's 1999 film *Eyes Wide Shut*. The camisole's cameo in the film caused sales of the Hanro camisole to skyrocket.

HOW TO ROCK IT: Despite their penchant for line-backer-size shoulder pads and fierce, frosted makeup, the working women of the '80s got one thing right—they knew how to wear a camisole. Follow their lead, and throw a suit jacket over a camisole, buttoning the jacket so that the camisole just peeks out the top.

Camisole

CHEMISE

WHAT IT LOOKS LIKE:
The chemise (pronounced "shim-meez") is a **slip**, traditionally made of linen or cotton, that possesses no form-fitting features (like darts or tapering) so it hangs straight from the shoulders. Today, just about any short, loose slip is described as a chemise.

Chemise

WHO MADE IT: The chemise was the most popular type of underwear in the 1700s. It was worn under **corsets**, crinolines, and petticoats to keep scratchy fabrics (like wool) from irritating the skin.

WHO MADE IT HOT: After leaving the world of modeling, ultimate LA woman Cindy Crawford etched out her personal style by pairing short, silky lace-trimmed chemises with jeans in the '90s.

HOW TO ROCK IT: Because of its loose cut, the chemise is the most comfortable option for sleepwear. If you dare to take your chemise to the street, wear it with pants to avoid overexposure.

The Weighty Business of Underwear

Getting dressed used to be such a chore that it required the help of someone else to complete the task. Like Kirsten Dunst in Sofia Coppola's 2006 film *Marie Antoinette* and Kate Winslet in James Cameron's 1997 *Titanic*, ladies of the late 18th and early 19th centuries spent more time getting into their underwear than we do getting a haircut. Right up until the end of the 19th century, women piled on girdles, **stockings**, **corsets**, crinolines, petticoats, and smocklike **chemises** — and *then* put on a dress. Around the 1870s, the average woman's daily underwear ensemble weighed 7 to 10 pounds. That's like walking around with a 17-inch laptop strapped to your body. And you thought those granny panties were excessive!

CORSET

WHAT IT LOOKS LIKE: This tightening mechanism laces up in the front or the back along the bodice to help emphasize the waist. Traditional corsets featured whalebone inserts along the panels to help hold its stiff shape. A more modern and breathable version of the corset is the corslette, which is cut higher on the hips to provide the wearer a greater range of movement and instead of boning has more comfortable elastic panels.

WHO MADE IT: Corsets are one of the oldest and most painful garments in underwear history. Ready-made corsets hit the streets around the 1830s and became wildly popular, but both American and British physicians warned wearers of the health problems—like the crushing and displacement of internal organs and curvature of the spine—that could result from lacing a corset too tight. They are also simply hard to breathe in. The less-restricting corslette came onto the scene in the 1920s.

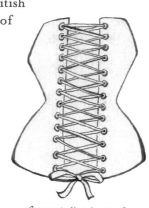

Corset (back view)

WHO MADE IT HOT: After a long absence from the fashion scene, corsets were revived by Vivienne Westwood in 1987. Madonna also famously wore corsets in her Blonde Ambition and Reinvention tours.

HOW TO ROCK IT: The corset isn't just tough on the body, but tough to pull off in everyday fashion. For a special night on the town, try lacing one up with a **pencil skirt** like Rhianna did at Kanye West's birthday party in 2007. For a more low-key event, the comfier corslette looks sharp and sexy under fitted **blazers**.

DEMI BRA

WHAT IT LOOKS LIKE: This push-up-style bra has wide-set straps and covers the breasts to only just above the nipple. Often, it's made with underwire to support the breasts.

WHO MADE IT: The demi bra evolved from everyday demi **corsets** (circa 1830) which offered the same partial coverage.

WHO MADE IT HOT: Marilyn Monroe gave the low-cut style its sexy image in the '50s. Today, steam queen Dita Von Teese often wears demi bras when performing her world-famous burlesque routines.

HOW TO ROCK IT: The demi works well with superlow scoop necks. Because of its partial coverage, this bra is best on small- or medium-busted ladies—larger breasts can fall victim to nip slips and boob overboard situations.

Demi Bra

FISHNETS

WHAT THEY LOOK LIKE: These **stockings** have a criss-cross mesh weave pattern, like a fisherman's net.

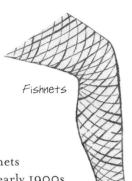

Fishnets

WHO MADE THEM: Fishnets arrived in the US in the early 1900s via Paris and later became a sensation among the flappers of the 1920s.

WHO MADE THEM HOT: Fishnets were given new life by Broadway's high-kicking chorus girls in productions like *Chicago* and *Cabaret* and the girls of the punk era.

HOW TO ROCK THEM: Fishnets can go from chic to skank when paired with a too-short hemline. To turn down the tramp factor trade the **hot pants** for a **pencil skirt** or other conservative clothes, like the sensible separates Maggie Gyllenhaal wore in *Secretary*. For a more demure look, try fishnet socks peeking out from jeans with **ballerina flats**.

FRENCH CUT BRIEFS

WHAT THEY LOOK LIKE: These **briefs** are cut super-high on the sides to elongate the leg.

WHO MADE THEM: The French cut brief was introduced in the early '80s as a more flattering variation of regular briefs.

French Cut Briefs

WHO MADE THEM HOT: The ladies of *Baywatch* flaunted seriously sexy French cut beachwear.

HOW TO ROCK THEM: To keep them hidden, these undies are best worn with dresses or high-cut pants and thick fabrics, like denim or wool.

HALF SLIP

WHAT IT LOOKS LIKE: A half slip is simply the skirt section of a full slip that fits from the waist to the thigh, knee, or calf.

WHO MADE IT: The half slip was a natural descendent of the full slip to serve the skirt-wearing set of the 1960s.

Half Slip

WHO MADE IT HOT: Anne Bancroft famously wore a leopard print bra and half slip while seducing a young Dustin Hoffman in *The Graduate*.

HOW TO ROCK IT: Thanks to the underwear-as-outerwear trend of the '90s, it's perfectly acceptable to layer two or three half slips of slightly varying lengths and wear them out as a skirt. Half slips also work for their original intent, of course—to add a liner to sheer skirts. If you're going for a natural look, make sure your half slip hits about an inch above your hemline and that the slip matches the flesh tone of your skin, not the color of the skirt's fabric.

HIPSTER BRIEFS

WHAT THEY LOOK LIKE:
These **briefs** hit superlow
at the waist to complement
low-rise jeans. They are cut
slightly higher on the leg
than a **boy brief.**

WHO MADE THEM: Some
of the first hipster designers, including London streetwear
designer Mary Quant, made versions
of hipster briefs in the '60s. By 1972,
they were in huge demand.

Hipster Briefs

WHO MADE THEM HOT: Before becoming
known for wearing no underwear at all, Britney
Spears squeezed into nothing but hipsters on the
October 2003 cover of *Rolling Stone* magazine.

HOW TO ROCK THEM: Hipsters are a great
undie option for **low-rise jeans**—and they go
well with a **camisole** for bedtime or for just
lounging around your room.

Knee-Highs

KNEE-HIGHS

WHAT THEY LOOK LIKE: These
abbreviated stay-up **stockings,** made of
nylon or sock material, extend to right
below the knee.

WHO MADE THEM: The knee-high was
launched in the 1950s as an alternative to
waist-hugging **pantyhose.**

WHO MADE THEM HOT: Pierre Cardin's
space-age dresses of the '60s were often
paired with knee-highs. Off-beat screen queens
like Thora Birch in *Ghost World* have often put
knee-highs with vintage minidresses.

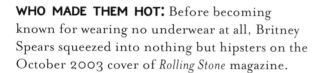

HOW TO ROCK THEM: Knee-highs offer a
pantyhose effect without the constricting band
of elastic wrapped around the waist. Sheer styles
work great with **trousers** or calf-length skirts
and heels. Knee-highs made of opaque **tights**
material are a great match for shorter skirts
and **Mary Janes.**

LEGGINGS

WHAT THEY LOOK LIKE:
Leggings are a thicker,
pantslike version of opaque
tights that stop at the ankle
or above.

WHO MADE THEM: Science
is credited with helping spur
this tights-as-pants trend. In
1959, DuPont created Lycra,
a spandex fiber that can stretch
more than 500 percent and still retain its original shape. At first, Lycra was used in bras and
pantyhose, but by 1978, spandex leggings ruled
the streets and roller discos alike.

Leggings

WHO MADE THEM HOT: In the '80s, Madonna
and Demi Moore were leggings queens, wearing them in music videos and even to the
Academy Awards (ouch!). In more recent
times, Sienna Miller, Kirsten Dunst, Lindsay
Lohan, and nearly every girl in Hollywood
has helped rekindle the romance with stretch,
wearing leggings with everything from **T-shirts**
to retro-rific **tent dresses.**

HOW TO ROCK THEM: Leggings can make
an otherwise iffy outfit instantly acceptable.
Wear them when your skirts or dresses are
short enough to show your rear or sheer
enough to show it *all.*

LEOTARD
(AKA BODYSUIT)

WHAT IT LOOKS LIKE: A leotard looks like a scoop-necked one-piece bathing suit with sleeves. It is sometimes also known as a bodysuit or unitard.

Leotard
(AKA Bodysuit)

WHO MADE IT: In 1859, gymnast Jules Leotard invented the trapeze. While his flying invention garnered oohhs and ahhhs, it was the outfit—the leotard—he designed to wear while performing that left the biggest impression.

WHO MADE IT HOT: Jane Fonda single-handedly started the leotard craze of the 1980s when she wore a rainbow of leotards in her best-selling workout tapes. In the '90s, grungified waifs wore bodysuits (leotards that are often equipped with snaps at the crotch) under shrunken dresses. And in 2005, the mother of reinvention, Madonna, made the leotard iconic again when she rocked a purple number on the cover of her *Confessions on a Dance Floor* album.

HOW TO ROCK IT: Though they make trips to the loo a bit more involved, bodysuits and leotards are great pieces for layering. Rock one under a **jumper dress**, like trendsetters in the '40s and '90s did.

PADDED BRA

WHAT IT LOOKS LIKE: This famous bra style is armored with extra padding in the cups to smooth the boob, make it appear a bit bigger, and conceal nipples.

WHO MADE IT: The buxom film stars of the '50s, armed with their torpedo bras, sparked a national trend in flaunting pointy padded bust lines. By 1957, the so-called sweater bra emerged from this trend and became the most popular style of brassiere. Padded bras continued to take off in the '60s.

WHO MADE IT HOT: For her title role in the 2000 film *Erin Brockovich*, Julia Roberts famously wore a gel-filled bra that both padded and pushed the cleavage together for in-your-face results.

HOW TO ROCK IT: Be careful wearing padded bras with wispy **T-shirts**; some can have a thick cupline that shows a bump (where the bra ends and your skin begins) right through your shirt. Instead, pair your padded bra with a sweater like the screen sirens of the '50s and '60s did, or go for a full-cup design to minimize show-through lines.

Padded Bra

PANTYHOSE

WHAT THEY LOOK LIKE:
Pantyhose are **stockings** with an elastic waist-band and provide sheer coverage from the waist to the toes.

WHO MADE THEM:
Inventor Allen E. Gant is credited with invent-ing pantyhose (or what he then dubbed Panti-Legs) in 1959, but like many good inventions, it was a woman's idea in the first place. In 1953, after pregnancy made her too wide to wear her garter, Gant's wife Ethel sewed together a prototype of stockings with panties attached.

WHO MADE THEM HOT: When Mary Quant made the **miniskirt** popular in the 1960s, the sales of pantyhose really took off. Suddenly, miniskirt-rocking hipsters needed *some* coverage to help hide hair, veins, and discoloration on their legs.

HOW TO ROCK THEM: Pantyhose aren't reserved just for career women, whose uniforms can often include pantyhose with skirt suits. Though our genera-tion is blessed with the free-form comfort of casual dress-ing, pantyhose still rule with formal attire.

Pantyhose

Good-Bye Girdle, Hello 'Hose

For generations of women, girdles were a part of daily dress. Though this circulation killer was uncomfortable to wear, women relied on the undergarment's slimming effect. But by the 1970s, the desire to squeeze into a constricting girdle diminished consider-ably—thanks to the rise of casual dress, the craze to keep fit, and the simple function that **pantyhose** played by both holding up **stockings** and helping to smooth and slim the body with its control top. In the mid-'70s, polls showed that more than half of women under the age of 34 wouldn't be caught dead in a girdle.

PRINCESS SLIP

WHAT IT LOOKS LIKE: This long **slip** is cut close to the body and flares out near the knees.

WHO MADE IT: The princess slip became pop-ular in the 1930s, though its shape stemmed from the petticoats named in honor of Princess Alexandra of Wales in the 1860s. After WWI, the princess petticoat became known as the princess slip.

WHO MADE IT HOT: Television actress Jorja Fox, star of *CSI*, brought the princess slip out of obscurity when she wore a pink princess slip dress with pearls to the 2004 Emmys.

HOW TO ROCK IT: Despite what your grandma says, a slip that peeks out from under a dress or skirt can look great. Try wearing a princess slip that flares with pleats under a slightly shorter **slip dress**.

Princess Slip

PUSH-UP BRA

WHAT IT LOOKS LIKE:
This bra is engineered to create cleavage by using side padding to push the breasts together.

Push-Up Bra

WHO MADE IT: Push-up bras can be traced as far back as 1893, but they really came into the lime-light in 1943, when billionaire Howard Hughes engineered a push-up for ingénue Jane Russell to wear in *The Outlaw*. This was a publicity stunt to draw attention to the new star and her, ahem, assets. Though it's likely that she did wear some sort of boob-enhancing bra in the movie, Jane Russell claimed she never wore it—implying her most-known feature was all real.

WHO MADE IT HOT: The most famous push-up bra, the Wonderbra, was created by Canadian designer Louise Poirier in 1964. It wasn't until 1994 that the brand brought its bra stateside, along with a multimillion-dollar advertising campaign starring supermodel Eva Herzigova and plenty of media hype. Within days of its arrival, several stores completely sold out of the bra, which even had the endorsement of famously flat-chested Kate Moss (she declared it to be "brilliant" in the April 1994 issue of *Vanity Fair* magazine).

HOW TO ROCK IT: Because this bra is such a great cleavage maker, it looks best with V-neck sweaters and low-cut tops.

RACER-BACK BRA
(AKA V-BACK BRA)

WHAT IT LOOKS LIKE: This bra's straps are designed with a halter style that meets to form a T in the back. It usually features a front closure.

WHO MADE IT:
Underwear companies introduced the racer-back bra in the mid-1980s to accommodate **tank tops** with oversize armholes.

*Racer-Back Bra
(AKA V-Back Bra)*

How the Bra Was Born

The development of the bra was no over-night success. Here are highlights from the 70-year span in which the "bust bodice" became the "bra."

1863 to 1900 ● Breast supporters, bust extenders, bust shapers, corset waists, and bust bodices are created, patented, and marketed as alternatives to corsets.

1905 ● *Vogue* magazine introduces the term *brassiere.*

WHO MADE IT HOT: In the 2004 film *Million Dollar Baby*, a muscular Hilary Swank boxed her way to championships in racer-back tops and **sports bras**.

HOW TO ROCK IT: If you're going for a clean look—no bra straps hanging out—then wear the racer back with racer-back tops, like **A-shirts**, and dresses cut to reveal the shoulder blades.

SHAPEWEAR

WHAT IT LOOKS LIKE: Shapewear—the name for all figure-hugging undergarments that suck it all in while creating smooth lines—comes in different styles, from **briefs** and **camisoles** to **slips** and bicycle shorts.

WHO MADE IT: Remember those archaic girdles our great-grandmothers wore? Shapewear is the updated version. The good news is that these garments are made of more modern and comfortable fabrics and don't feature the inflexible structure, like boning, that the girdle had.

WHO MADE IT HOT: Shapewear is Hollywood's dirty little secret. A-list actresses wear it beneath those gazillion-dollar dresses to give them gazillion-dollar shapes. While hitting the fashion shows with Victoria Beckham in 2007, Katie Holmes let her shapewear-covered thighs show when exiting a car.

HOW TO ROCK IT: Shapewear's signature spandex and Lycra has a slimming and smoothing effect on virtually any body part, which can be a godsend when it comes to wearing body-skimming dresses. Shapewear undies and slips can make the tummy appear more toned, while bike shorts can keep thighs held tight. Just don't get carried away with shapewear's slimming possibilities and don sizes that are way too small. Beauty is beauty and pain is pain—you should be able to breathe in your undies.

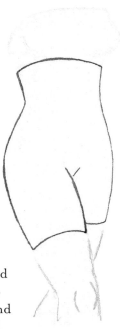

Shapewear

1914 ❶ Mary Phelps Jacob patents her design for the brassiere. Underwear company Warners purchases the patent the same year.

1918 to 1929 ❷ Nearly 200 patents are granted for brassiere and corslette designs, but they are far from perfect. The straps aren't yet adjustable, and delicate fabrics like silk and rayon are prone to snagging.

1932 ❸ Separate brassiere makers introduce the band measurements (32, 34, 36 inches measured around the rib cage) and cup sizing system (A, B, C, D) that we still use today.

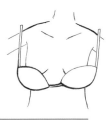

1934 ❹ The slang term "bra" (mostly used by college kids) replaces stuffy-sounding "brassiere" as the hot new word for the latest thing in ladies underwear.

SLIP
(AKA FULL SLIP)

WHAT IT LOOKS LIKE: The standard slip generally has a bralike top and bias cut and falls past the knees.

WHO MADE IT: Slips of the 1920s were crudely cut in a straight line, with no darts to complement the bust-line. By the 1930s, they began to resemble the slips of today. They were often cut on the bias and featured shaping features, like darting near the breasts.

Slip
(AKA Full Slip)

WHO MADE IT HOT: Elizabeth Taylor famously donned a slip in *Cat on a Hot Tin Roof* when vying for the attention of Paul Newman, her onscreen alcoholic husband. In both the 1933 and 2005 *King Kong* films, the blond heroine screamed her way through the jungle in nothing but a slip.

HOW TO ROCK IT: Slips do wonders under knits and other clingy fabrics. They also keep your form smooth and your dress from bunching up or sticking to the back of your legs when you move.

SPORTS BRA

WHAT IT LOOKS LIKE: A sports bra is simply a cotton Lycra **bandeau** with straps made for keeping your breasts in place while playing sports.

Sports Bra

WHO MADE IT: In 1977, two women developed a bra they could run in by tweaking a couple of deconstructed jockstraps. Dubbed the Jogbra, it had no metal parts, a fat elastic band, and criss-cross straps. As the workout trend surged in the '80s, underwear companies jumped on board the Jogbra train and developed similar sports bras to keep breasts from bouncing *Baywatch*-style.

WHO MADE IT HOT: After a game-winning penalty kick in the 1999 Women's World Cup, soccer star Brandi Chastain ripped off her shirt and fell to her knees in excitement, giving the sports bra the most exposure in its history.

HOW TO ROCK IT: Generally, it's worn while playing sports or doing yoga, but in a pinch, a sports bra can double as a bathing suit top for unexpected dips in the pool.

Stockings
(AKA Stay-Ups)

STOCKINGS
(AKA STAY-UPS)

WHAT THEY LOOK LIKE: Traditional stockings were thigh-high **pantyhose** that were attached to a garter belt with clips. But in the mid-'80s, a new kind of stocking was introduced—the hold-up. Also called stay-ups and thigh-highs, these stockings feature elastic, rubber, or silicone bands at the thigh that are designed to adhere to the leg and stay put without the help of a garter belt. Today, both types of stockings remain popular.

WHO MADE THEM: Though stockings were worn in Egypt as far back as 650 CE, the 1589 advent

of the knitting frame, a machine that knits fibers together, made stockings more available and popular than ever. Wool, silk, and rayon were used to make stockings up until 1938, when nylons, made of DuPont's freshly patented material nylon, were first introduced in the US.

WHO MADE THEM HOT: The ladies of the "naughty nineties" (1890s, that is) made stockings look especially sexy when they performed the cancan—a dance that demanded a high kick and a flash of stockings, garters, and **briefs**. Clara Bow, the original "It Girl" of the '20s, was known for wearing her stockings rolled down. Modern-day sex pots including the Pussycat Dolls, Paris Hilton, and Christina Aguilera have all rocked stockings with exposed garter belt clips.

HOW TO ROCK THEM: Stockings are a great option for the girl who doesn't want to feel constricted by control-top pantyhose. When wearing stockings with garters, be mindful of your skirt length—it's nearly impossible to wear a micromini with peek-through garter clips and not look like a stripper. If you're wearing stay-ups, skip the lotion—it makes the silicone and rubber slip away from the skin. And wear them around the house first to make sure they are secure; you don't want to be stuck at a party with a **miniskirt** and saggy stockings.

String Bikini

STRING BIKINI

WHAT IT LOOKS LIKE:
A string bikini is a **bikini brief** with thin, stringy straps that connect the front and back panels.

WHO MADE IT: In the mid-1970s, string bikinis were the uniforms of dancers who performed at cabarets like the Crazy Horse Saloon in Paris. The style was introduced to lingerie shops and, by 1984, Calvin Klein's and Jockey's best-sellers were string bikinis.

WHO MADE IT HOT: In the '90s, supermodels like Kate Moss and Christy Turlington wore nothing but tiny **tanks** and string bikinis in their famous Calvin Klein underwear ads.

HOW TO ROCK IT: String bikinis are a great in-betweener to the **thong** and **French cut brief** since they can look sexy without overdoing it. Because they have minimal fabric on the sides, they're a nice match for lace-up **leather pants** or skirts.

TEDDY

WHAT IT LOOKS LIKE:
This one-piece undergarment merges little shorts or **briefs** with a **chemise** or **camisole** top. When first invented, teddies were somewhat baggy and loose in construction, but over the years, the teddy has evolved to resemble a racy one-piece bathing suit with higher-cut bottoms.

Teddy

WHO MADE IT: Theodore Baer invented his namesake undergarment in the 1920s.

WHO MADE IT HOT: Playboy bunnies wore their trademark strapless teddies while waiting tables at the legendary New York Playboy Club in the 1960s.

HOW TO ROCK IT: Lucky for us, we typically wear easygoing cotton separates, so there's not much of a need for full-coverage one-piece undergarments. Now people just wear teddies to feel sexy.

THONG (AKA TANGA)

WHAT IT LOOKS LIKE: This barely there underwear looks like a run-of-the-mill **string bikini** on the front, but turn it around and you'll see just an inch-or-so strip of fabric to cover the upper backside, near the top of the crack. The thong's close relative, the G-string, is even more scant—the verticle and horizontal lines meet with no additional fabric coverage in back.

WHO MADE IT: The thong is a spin-off of the Brazilian string bikini. Its origins in the US can be traced to 1939, when nude dancers in New York City started wearing these little undies to pacify the mayor (who asked that they cover up while the World Fair was in town). Designer Rudi Gerneich, a West Coast designer, patented the first thong in 1979.

Thong (AKA Tanga)

WHO MADE IT HOT: The popularity of the thong really took off in the early 2000s, as women began pairing high-rise thong straps with ultra-**low-rise jeans**. In 1998, Halle Berry's character in *Bulworth* strutted around with her pants sagging to reveal her thong. Pop tarts Mariah Carey and Britney Spears followed, and soon Sisqo sealed the deal with his radio hit, "The Thong Song."

HOW TO ROCK IT: Although the thong's be-tween-the-bum fit might seem extreme to some, it's a great way to ensure you don't show VPL without going commando. Still, despite what Mariah and other thong-exhibitionists may have done, underwear hanging out of your pants is not a good look—unless you're dressing for Halloween. Instead, keep your undies under wraps by pairing them with dresses or higher-waisted pants, not low-rise jeans.

TIGHTS

WHAT THEY LOOK LIKE: Tights are a thicker, opaque version of **pantyhose**.

Tights

WHO MADE THEM: Colorful **stockings** were a normal part of dress in the 1860s, but the thick tights we wear today came onto the scene in the 1960s and were inspired by a winter wear trend like long johns. As **miniskirts** and rising hemlines became all the rage in the '60s and '70s, tights helped to keep a little warmth—and conservatism—on the streets.

WHO MADE THEM HOT: Edie Sedgwick brought tights to the spotlight when pairing them with nothing but a **T-shirt** in her mid-'60s factory girl days. Fashion wunderkinds Mary Kate and Ashley Olsen nicked Sedgwick's look and have since become famous for wearing tights with grandma sweaters, scarves, and heels.

HOW TO ROCK THEM: For a fiercely preppy look, do like Winona Ryder and crew in the 1989 flick *Heathers* and rock tights with miniskirts and **blazers**.

T-SHIRT BRA (AKA SEAMLESS BRA)

WHAT IT LOOKS LIKE: This bra has no seams across the front of its cups; instead, the seam is at the upper edge, giving full and butter-smooth coverage.

WHO MADE IT: Seamless bras and panties were developed in the early '70s by Olga Erteszek, founder of the Olga underwear company, to be worn with slinky disco fabrics like lamme that dominated street fashion.

WHO MADE IT HOT: Models like Gisele Bundchen steamed up the small screen and made the most matronly of modern-day bras look ultrasexy in Victoria's Secret Body By Victoria ad campaign.

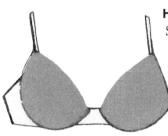

T-Shirt Bra (AKA Seamless Bra)

HOW TO ROCK IT: Since this bra is so smooth, and often made in skintones, it's a great choice for the girl who likes to wear extra-fine cotton **T-shirts** or other sheer woven tops.

UNDERWIRE BRA

WHAT IT LOOKS LIKE: This wardrobe staple for many is a bra with built-in U-shaped wires along the cups that help shape breasts and provide support. Most **padded bras**, and lots of un-padded bras, come with underwires.

WHO MADE IT: Because **corsets** were structured with bone and wire, the progression to building an underwire bra was a natural one. Underwire bras first appeared in the late '30s and became very popular in the push-up crazed '50s. They didn't get the name underwire until after the '60s, when nonwire bras, such as Rudi Gerneich's famous "no-bra bra" came onto the scene.

Underwire Bra

WHO MADE IT HOT: Buxom babe Brigitte Bardot was famous for wearing bikini bathing suits with underwire bra tops in the '60s. The full-support bra became a big hit for women wanting to capture Bardot's sex kitten allure.

HOW TO ROCK IT: Underwire bras are great for girls with small breasts; they are also helpful in giving structure to breasts that sag. Because of the way they help shape you, they work well under snug-fitting tops and dresses. Just be sure yours fits right. If you feel the underwire digging into the side or resting on top of your boob, you should be wearing the next larger size.

Size Matters

According to industry experts, between 70 and 85 percent of women wear the wrong bra size. Not only can this make a great outfit look bad, but ill-fitting bras can also cause rashes and other skin problems. To avoid the trap of falling straps, breasts that spill over, or cups that sag, try the following tips:

❶ If the band in back sits higher than the bottom of the bra, try a bra with a tighter band.

❷ If your skin is bulging out the sides or back, try a bra with a bigger band.

❸ Most women have one boob that's bigger than the other; make sure to tighten the strap that corresponds with the smaller boob.

❹ If the cups of your bra are saggy, move down a cup size.

❺ As you gain and lose weight, go on and off birth control, or have your period, your bra size will change. Be prepared to buy bras accordingly. When in doubt, visit a specialty lingerie shop and ask to get fitted.

ABOUT THE CONTRIBUTORS

Erika Stalder is a San Francisco-based writer who has contributed to *Wired*, *Missbehave*, and *The Journal of Life Sciences*, and worked with the International Museum of Women to produce the *Imagining Ourselves* anthology. She also wrote *The Date Book: A Teen Girl's Guide to Going Out With Someone New* and coauthored 97 *Things to Do Before You Finish High School*.

Ariel Krietzman, 20, is a graduate of the School of the Arts high school in San Francisco where she majored in theater design. She currently attends Knox College in Galesburg, Illinois, and is pursuing a degree in fine arts. She has experience in costume design, knitting, art welding, and pottery. This is her first professional illustration project.

Thank You:

Jeff Baumgardner	Maple Porter
Beth Kita	Pennie Rossini, copy editor
Diane Kwan	Rachel Shaw
Rob Larsen	Rebecca Smith Hurd
Melissa Miller	FIDM Library, San Francisco
Eleni Nicholas	The Bata Shoe Museum, Toronto
Daniel Draves Parker, photography	Museum of Bags and Purses, Amsterdam
Steven Pavlopoulos	River and Rowing Museum, Henley on Thames